Σάν βγε

νά εὔχεσα

γεμάτος

Τούς Λαι

Τόν θυ

Clearing the Ground

Clearing the Ground

C. P. CAVAFY

Poetry and Prose, 1902–1911

Edited, Translated, and with an Essay by Martin McKinsey

Laertes

Chapel Hill, North Carolina

Printed in the United States of America

First edition

Cover and book design by Maxine Mills

The cover painting is based on a photograph taken in 1910, now preserved in the Cavafy Archive. Used throughout are details from original manuscript pages, given here as "Philosophical Scrutiny," "September 1903," "An Object of Speculation," "On Writing and the Erotic," "Ithaca," and "A *Discipline de Vie*." They are in the Cavafy Archive's care as well.

PUBLISHER CATALOGING-IN-PUBLICATION DATA

Cavafy, Constantine, 1863-1933
[Selections. English. 2015]
Clearing the ground: C. P. Cavafy, poetry and prose 1902-1911/
edited, translated, and with an essay by Martin McKinsey.
pages cm.

Includes bibliographical references

ISBN 978-1-942281-00-9 (softcover : alk. paper)

1. Cavafy, Constantine, 1863-1933 — Translations into English.
2. Cavafy, Constantine, 1863-1933 — Criticism and Interpretation.

I. McKinsey, Martin. II. Title

PA5610.K2 A2 2015
889'.832-dc23
Library of Congress Control Number: 2014959310

Laertes a press for literary translation

www.laertesbooks.org

I know that I am cowardly, and am unable to act. Therefore I confine myself to words. But I don't think that my words are without purpose. Someone else will act. But my many words — the words of a coward — will make it easier for that person to act. My words clear the ground.

Constantine Cavafy, 1902

CONTENTS

1908

1909

1910

1911

I. INTRODUCTION

Among the 75 poems that Cavafy chose to leave unpublished during his lifetime—excluding the 30 that he left unfinished at his death—is one entitled "The rest I will tell to those below in Hades," written in 1898 and revised in 1912. The poem imagines a brief exchange between a Roman proconsul and a (presumably) Greek sophist, as they discuss a passage from ancient tragedy.

> "Indeed," said the proconsul, putting the book down,
> "that line is beautiful, and so very true:
> Sophocles at his most profound.
> How many things we shall say below!
> And how different we'll appear.
> All the things we stand guard over here,
> injuries and secrets we keep locked away
> with such anxiety, day after day,
> there we shall freely and openly tell."
>
> "Assuming," added the sophist with a wry smile,
> "that people talk about such matters there,
> that anyone still cares about them there."

The proconsul muses out loud on a line from Sophocles's *Ajax* quoted in the title, which represents the Greek hero's last words before he takes his own life. Inspired by Ajax's line, the Roman official wishfully envisions the afterlife as a place free from societal constraints, an age of transparency when the things kept hidden in this world will be freely revealed, and humans will be seen as they truly are.

Given that Cavafy, as a homosexual living in the early twentieth century, had more than his share of things to keep "locked away" in his breast and, as a writer, in his drawer, it seems fair to identify the proconsul's "secrets" on some level with Cavafy's own. By extension, they can be identified with the

Κρυμμένα or "hidden writings"—as Cavafy's posthumous works have come to be known in Greece—which make up the better part of this book, and which are often revealing in ways his published writing and public utterances were not. Viewed in this light, the sophist's wry comment in the second stanza—*if* anyone cares about such matters anymore—is all the more germane, because the question it raises is one we can imagine Cavafy asking about his own work. What would people of the future care about his writings, "hidden" or otherwise, after he was gone?

Now, a century later, the answer is clear: they care quite a bit. In Greece, Cavafy is seen as a national treasure, perhaps the most valued modern contributor to a tradition that goes back to Sophocles and beyond; but even abroad he has found his niche in the pantheon of modern poetry. A recent trip to the two major bookstores in Harvard Square revealed, respectively, four and five different versions of Cavafy's poems on the shelves—an honor accorded, as far as my quick survey went, not even to Dante or Homer.

Writing in 1959, in the afterword to his novel *Justine*, Lawrence Durrell remarked that the first collected edition of Cavafy's poems in English, by John Mavrogordato, had "freed" him to "experiment" in his own versions of two of the poems.[1] How much more true this is today! The plethora of existing "complete" editions—variously defined—has freed me to experiment in the present book with a different notion of completeness. In *Clearing the Ground* I have gone for depth rather than breadth, for portrait rather than landscape. And a portrait of sorts is what emerges in this book: the portrait of an artist slowly, in his forties, coming into his own, establishing for himself, to borrow from one of the texts here, a "ground to stand on." The decade it covers—from 1902 to 1911—is not chosen at random. It begins immediately following a period of unspecified crisis during the years 1898 to 1901, and ends with the ambivalent arrival signaled by the poem "Ithaca" published in 1911: the year that for Cavafy marked the "before" and "after" of his creative development. It is a period regarded as providing the key to Cavafy's emergence as a master poet of "passions and

1. Lawrence Durrell, *Justine* (New York: Penguin, 1991), 251.

ancient days." "Cavafy wasn't born a poet," wrote fellow Alexandrian I. A. Sareyannis, "he became one over the years. He found his final form in 1911." This book undertakes to show how that came about.

This volume presents in chronological arrangement the better part of what Cavafy wrote during this ten-year span, both in verse and in prose, both published and unpublished. The reader will thus find "canonical" and "hidden" poems juxtaposed and intermingled with short notes in prose on sexuality, language, and society, and longer pieces on literature, publishing, and poetics. My practical aim in taking such an approach is to see what new picture might emerge of the poet and his work from this textually dense bricolage, within which I strive for a relative comprehensiveness. My primary criteria for inclusion have been the following, in no particular order:

1) availability of a reliable Greek text for translation;

2) importance of the material to Cavafy's creative development;

3) potential interest to English-language readers.

These criteria coincide loosely with a fourth category: works Cavafy committed to paper with potential readers—present or future—in mind. This distinction is most easily perceived in the clean drafts Cavafy left behind of most of the unpublished texts here (though even these show signs of later revision).

The poems are drawn from Cavafy's collected poems or "canon"—those he chose to print and preserve—and from the posthumous "hidden" poems. None of the prose included from the period was published during his lifetime (Cavafy's aspirations as a writer of prose largely ended with the turn of the century).[2] The bulk of it consists of the so-called "Notes on Poetics and Ethics"; in fact, it is this series of speculative jottings dating from 1902 to 1911—none much more than a page, most no more than a paragraph—that has provided the chronological frame as well as inspiration for this

2. Two published pieces from the period are not included: a minor review of a collection by the poet Markos Avyeris, and a brief appreciation of the prose writer Alexandros Papadiamandis.

volume.[3] Taken together, the Notes represent possibly the single most interesting prose Cavafy ever wrote. Halfway between journal entry and philosophical *pensée*, between private confession and public pronouncement, they address both abstract issues of social existence—thus the label "ethical"—and the concrete concerns of Cavafy the writer, often though not exclusively touching on the theme of writing and sexuality.

To these shorter pieces are added two slightly longer works in prose: the so-called "Philosophical Scrutiny" of 1903—a four-page personal manifesto in which the poet attempts to define the principles for a major review of his poems to date; and a brief unpublished essay from 1907 entitled "Independence" that finds a silver lining to the lamentable state of Greek publishing in Cavafy's day. Finally, an unfinished essay on the medieval verse narrative "The Chronicle of the Morea"—evidence that Cavafy's mind during this period, for all its cosmopolitan engagements, also roamed to thoughts of national culture—is included in the appendix.

The novelty of my approach is two-fold: first, its integration of poetry and prose, and second, its arrangement according to date of composition, rather than date of publication, or one of the several other principles that have been applied to his poetic works.[4] My aim is to allow the reader to follow Cavafy's development during this crucial decade—his period of "clearing the ground"—from month to month, and when possible from day to day. Cavafy is famous for often having delayed publishing his poems for many years, as he worked and reworked them and tested them against his severe standards of sincerity and accuracy (as laid out in the "Philosophical Scrutiny"), so that the dates of publication, while significant markers in the shaping of his canon, are less informative when it comes to his evolution as a poet. Cavafy was nothing if not fastidious—truly English in his fondness for recordkeeping—and

3. The texts of the "Notes" are those edited by G. P. Savidis and first published in 1983. See G. P. Savidis, *Short Writings on Cavafy*, vol. 2. (Athens: Ermis, 1987). The texts of the remaining prose come from *The Prose*, edited by Mihalis Pieris (Athens: Ikaros, 2003).

4. These include thematic, published/unpublished, collected/rejected. One translator manages to divide the poems alone into eight distinct categories.

maintained a meticulous running account of his poetic efforts, recording dates of composition as well as of rewriting. Most of the Notes included here are dated to the day. While Cavafy's Greek editor, G. P. Savidis, warns against the pitfalls of attempting a chronological arrangement of the poems,[5] it is Savidis's own careful sorting and notating of Cavafy's records that make this book possible. In the few cases where precise dating isn't available, I have fallen back on instinct and intuition, the translator's prerogative. In at least one instance, my reading of the catalogues has differed from that of Savidis.

Two important sets of writing have been left out, though they are given due attention in the Afterword: the so-called "self-commentaries" and the so-called "confessional notes." My principal reason for not including them is practical: no reliable or complete edition has yet appeared in Greece, in large part due to the challenge of deciphering and decoding the shorthand in which most of them are written. The self-commentaries were either a product of the "Scrutiny" process, or written in response to his brother John's fascinating if often misguided attempts to translate Constantine's poems into English.[6] Many of the commentaries refer to poems preceding this period; many others were written after 1911 (dating of these notes is problematic); and many are simply not yet available for translation, so that it seems wisest to exclude them altogether. One advantage of leaving them out is that the textual portrait that emerges here is less cluttered with references to poems outside our period, though it is worth remembering that Cavafy was still occupied with these earlier efforts—often in the Symbolist mode—throughout the decade.

The "confessional notes" present their own set of issues. Chronologically they overlap with the "Notes on Poetics and Ethics," and so with our period.

---

5. "[A]ny attempt to arrange the 'Published Poems' in order of composition would not only be problematic but hopeless, particularly since the date of composition of most of the poems printed by Cavafy between 1925–1932 is unknown." George Savidis, "Editor's Introduction." *Collected Poems.* Edmund Keeley and Philip Sherrard, trans. (Princeton, NJ: Princeton University Press, 1975), 197.

6. I have included John Cavafy's English translation of "Orophernes," along with the poet's own prose rendering of "Satrapy" to give a sense of how these poems might have sounded in period English. John's translations are available online at http://www.cavafy.org.

They begin earlier—around 1897—but many if not most of them date from after the turn of the century, with the last one dated October 17, 1911. Again, the main reason for omitting them here is availability: only a handful have been published, and these in the unreliable form of undated paraphrase, or in Greek translation from unknown English originals written in shorthand. The confessional notes will no doubt appear in print someday; given the scattershot and unreliable state of those that have already appeared, this is probably for the best. Whether these private jottings truly belong in Cavafy's collected works is another matter. Fortunately, their material elusiveness has spared me that particular editorial quandary. I do, however, discuss them at length in my Afterword.

Of the recent material I do include, easily the most important is the "Notes on Poetics and Ethics." Not only do these supply me with a chronological frame, but one of them supplies me with a title for this book. As I said earlier, *Clearing the Ground* had its genesis in my curiosity to see what the effect would be if the Notes were transposed onto the poems from the same period. In fact, the effect is dramatic. The Notes bring sharply into focus the growing assertiveness of Cavafy's gay identity and his commitment to the process of artistic reinvention that to a degree came along with it. Some may feel that the Notes unfairly skew the book's emphasis toward the erotic poems, at the expense of the historical poems; after all, whereas antiquity is mentioned only once in the Notes, and then only in passing, the poetry itself is fairly balanced between the two. Among the historical poems written during this period we find some of his most memorable: "Satrapy," "Orophernes," "Philhellene," "Seleucid's Displeasure," "The God Abandons Antony." I am not the first to point out how difficult it is to keep these two categories apart, since sensuality and homoeroticism so thoroughly permeate Cavafy's vision of the ancient world, starting here with "A Crafter of Winebowls" of 1903 and ending with "Antiochus Epiphanes" of 1911. Still, there is no denying that my Afterword is principally concerned with matters sexual, and the role these played in the formation of Cavafy's poetics. But my approach to the subject is, I hope, open-ended and nondeterministic. As I discovered once I embarked on this project, the complexities and ambiguities of Cavafy's "breakthrough" are daunting. The last thing I want to suggest is a clean narrative of artistic becoming or sexual liberation of the sort others have hinted at before me. As Cavafy himself was acutely aware, life is more compromised and full of equivocation than that.

In the end, of course, readers won't need my help in detecting the rhythms and shifting configurations that emerge from page to page in the mixed poems and prose that follow; the connections they make and the conclusions they draw will be their own. The Afterword is my own attempt to justify and make sense of this particular collocation of texts, in a way that sheds light not just on the poems themselves, but on the processes of personal reckoning and artistic distillation that allowed Cavafy, years later, to refer to 1911 as a defining moment in his poetic coming-to-be.

A NOTE ON THE TRANSLATION

Cavafy's language is anything but transparent to a contemporary Greek reader of poetry. His idiom is uniquely his own, but also reflective of a number of social factors: the Alexandrian milieu in which he circulated, his family's Constantinopolitan roots (he spent several years in the Ottoman capital in his youth), the archaizing Katharevousa or Purist Greek in which he was schooled, and even, to a degree, the English in which he was more or less fluent (he'd spent formative years in England as a child), with occasional incursions from the Hellenistic or Byzantine Greek of his sources. This unlikely mix may strike a Greek ear as odd, even affected; but it would not strike it as awkward, at least in the works from 1900 onward. Cavafy was a patient re-worker of his poems, with a clear idea of the effects he was after. These involved a much discussed quality of voice that I will content myself here to label "Cavafian." But also involved were elements of pacing and rhythm—the movement of poem and voice—that belie claims about the "prose-like" quality of his verse. Through a combination of phrasing, enjambment, subtle assonance and measure (his favored meter was a very loose iambic), he achieved a form that reflected a carefully controlled movement of thought.

With the example of many worthy attempts before mine, I won't claim to have achieved in English anything like Cavafy's linguistic effects; these are too deeply rooted in the specific history of the Greek language and people, and of the Cavafy clan in particular. But his prosodic effects can, I believe, be conveyed, especially since they were shaped in part by his careful reading of English poetry. My translations attempt to be as semantically precise and tonally accurate as possible, without sacrificing the sure-footed movement of each line. I consider myself a Cavafy scholar, but these translations were not done primarily with scholars in mind, who presumably will have the Greek.

One peculiarity of this book is the inclusion of two translations by other hands. The hands are not just anyone's. They belong to Constantine and his older brother John, and their English versions are included to give a sense of how the poet and his closest confidant heard his poems in the English of their day. (Cavafy appears to have written his first verse in English, and John was a self-published poet in English as well as an enthusiastic translator of his brother's poems.) Neither of their versions—which to my knowledge have not appeared outside of Greece—is likely to become canonical, but they do convey a certain period flavor, and maybe something of the spirit of Cavafy's Greek; at the very least, their versions add to the multiplicity of voices through which these Greek poems can be heard in English.

My translations of the prose are based on the Greek texts in Michalis Pieris's edition of the *Prose* (Ikaros, 2003); and G. P. Savidis's edition of the Notes. I have mostly followed their rendering of Cavafy's abbreviations. In translating the prose, I tried for a certain fidelity to the period, using a diction loosely aligned with Cavafy's own English prose style, as seen in the "Philosophic Scrutiny" and in some of the Notes, as well as in the more formal writing (not included here) from before the turn of the century. I'd like to think that there is a certain continuity between his English prose and my own; that readers (my footnotes aside) might find themselves uncertain whose English they are reading on any given page. This happened to me more than once in the course of revising, and I'm encouraged by it.

ACKNOWLEDGMENTS

Two people in particular need to be thanked for their help with the translations. My longtime friend and unsung collaborator Elly Marmara pulled me back from the brink on numerous occasions and, thanks to her excellent English, provided solutions that often found their way into my finished versions. Thalia Pandiri of Smith College deserves mention for her scrupulous vetting of the full manuscript, and for catching a number of inconsistencies. The questions of another reader, Josiah Blackmore of Harvard University, helped me do a better job of explaining myself in the Afterword. I would also like to thank two Athens-based associates in Cavafy research, Diana Haas and Michaela Karabini-Iatrou, for sharing their detailed knowledge of Cavafy's life and writing. I have kept their scholarly examples in mind as a check to my more wayward impulses.

I am grateful to the Onassis Foundation and the Princeton University Program in Hellenic Studies for their generous support of this project, and to Manuel Savidis for permission to use material from the Cavafy Archive.

Finally, special thanks go to the publisher Nina Kamberos, whose encouragement and faith never faltered, even after the book took a direction neither of us expected.

II. POETRY AND PROSE, **1902–1911**

1902

[On Obsolete Words]

It is one of the talents of great stylists to make obsolete words cease from appearing obsolete through the way in which they introduce them in their writing. Obsolete words which under the pens of others would seem stilted or out of place, occur most naturally under theirs. This is owing to the tact & judgement of the writers who know when — & when only — the disused term can be introduced, when it is artistically agreeable or linguistically necessary; & of course then the obsolete word becomes obsolete only in name. It is recalled into existence by the natural requirements of a powerful or subtle style. It is not a corpse disinterred (as with less skillful writers) but a beautiful body awaked from a long & refreshing sleep.

[1902?]

~ This note is written in English.

[On Sincerity and Art]

Never in my life have I lived in the country. I haven't even made short visits to the countryside, as others do. And yet I wrote a poem in which I sing its praises, saying that my verses owe their very existence to it. The poem is scarcely deserving of note. Indeed, it would be difficult to imagine anything less sincere. An outright lie.

But now it occurs to me, — is this true insincerity? Doesn't art always lie? Or rather, isn't it that the more it lies, the more imaginative it becomes? When I wrote those lines, was it not a triumph of art? (That the verses themselves came out less than perfect may not have been due to the lack of sincerity; after all, how often one fails even with the benefit of the sincerest of poetic intuitions.) While I was composing the verses, did I not possess a certain artificial sincerity? Was not my imagining such that it was as if I had truly lived in the country?

7.5.1902

[On the Practical Professions]

I feel that I possess exceptional abilities. It is my conviction that if I chose, I could distinguish myself as a doctor, or a lawyer, or an economist, or even as an engineer. There are two things, however, that would be required: time to study, and the willpower to give up literature. Now, is this simply the intellect deceiving itself? Do I overrate my abilities? Or is it something that occurs naturally in littérateurs? — by which I mean, does every littérateur possess this facility? All endeavors of the practical kind seem easy to me. It is true that, for all my self-confidence, I recognize that without time — sufficient time — I should never be a success in the practical world. But assuming I were granted enough time, would I not then fall into the general category of humanity; since, with the expenditure of time, every individual, even someone of mediocre intelligence, is capable of succeeding. Or no; because what differentiates me from them is the consciousness that I would require far less time. This, however, does not blind me to the fact that I could never succeed in one of the practical professions, because I can't imagine — except through an effort that would all but break my spirit — ever rooting out the "hankering"* for literature in me. And here something else occurs to me. Perhaps this very ability of mine — which declares itself in the ease with which practical vocations come to me — itself derives from the literary life: from the endless thinking, from the "sharpening"* of the imagination. Were it possible for me to make the requisite effort, without doing injury to myself, and to forsake the Imagination, perhaps I would then lose these powers, and the practical vocation would present the same challenges to me as to the average man. But I don't believe this. The ability is there. My weakness — or we might call it my strength, if we dare suppose that creative endeavor has value — lies in my inability to renounce literature — or, more accurately, to renounce the voluptuous "agitation"* of the imagination.

8.18.1902

* In English in the original.

[On Truth and Falsehood]

Is there such a thing as Truth and Falsehood? Or is there only the New and the Old — and Falsehood simply the old age of Truth?

9.16.1902

[Clearing the Ground]

I often notice how little weight people give to words. Let me explain. A simple person (by simple I don't mean stupid — just not eminent) has an idea; he disapproves of an institution or disagrees with some widely held opinion; he is aware that the great majority holds a contrary view on the matter, therefore he keeps silent, seeing no point in speaking since his speaking would change nothing. This is a grave error. I behave differently. For example, I disapprove of capital punishment. Whenever an opportunity arises, I speak up, not because I believe that, on account of my saying something, governments are going to do away with the death penalty overnight, but because I am convinced that in speaking, I contribute to the ultimate victory of my view. It doesn't matter if anyone agrees with me. My words will not have been wasted. They may be repeated within hearing of someone else, who will take courage from them. Or perhaps one of those who at present disagrees with me will remember my words at an auspicious moment in the future and, in combination with other circumstances, might be led to change his mind, or at least have his conviction to the contrary shaken. And the same goes for a number of other social issues, including some that cry out for Action. I know that I am cowardly, and am unable to act. Therefore I confine myself to words. But I don't think that my words are without purpose. Someone else will act. But my many words — the words of a coward — will make it easier for that person to act. My words clear the ground.

10.19.1902

[A Single Letter]

It crossed my mind tonight to write about my love [*éros*] — but I'm not going to. What a powerful thing prejudice is! I have freed myself from it, but I think of those still enslaved to it who might chance to look upon this page — and I stop myself. What cowardliness. But let me note down a single letter — T — as a token of this moment.

11.9.1902

[Art and Arousal]

Who can say what libidinous thoughts govern the making of most literary works. Libidinous idées solitaires, that pervert (or transform) the conception. And how often in various novels (especially the English ones) those things with which the critics find fault — indeed some places where they are at a loss to explain the author's apparent deliberate badness — are due to the latter's forced subservience — while in the act of writing — to a sensation or condition of sexual arousal. This feeling is so powerful — and at times so poetic, so sublimely beautiful! — that it is inextricable from the words whose birth it accompanied. And the author, even reading them months later, is incapable of correcting or altering a thing, because the act of re-reading the passage calls up a simulacrum of the earlier sensation, thus rendering him "colour-blind,"* as it were, to a portion of his work.

11.12.1902

* In English in the original.

[Sexual Deviance]

I don't know whether sexual deviance makes one stronger. Sometimes I think so. But there is no question that it is the root of greatness.

12.13.1902

1903

PERFIDY

Then, although there are many things to praise in Homer, this we do not praise . . . nor [the verses] of Aeschylus, where Thetis says that Apollo at her nuptials

> *"was celebrating in song her fair progeny whose days were to be long, and to know no sickness. And when he had spoken of my lot as in all things blessed of heaven he raised a note of triumph and cheered my soul. And I thought that the word of Phoebus being divine and full of prophecy, would not fail. And now he himself who uttered the strain . . . he it is who has slain my son."*

Plato, The Republic, *Part 2*[1]

When Thetis and Peleus were joined in marriage,
Apollo stood up at the splendid wedding feast
and toasted the newlyweds for the son
that would issue from their union. Sickness,
he said, would never touch the boy,
and his life would be long. Hearing this,
Thetis inwardly rejoiced, for the words
of Apollo, who was gifted in prophecy,
seemed a surety for her child. And later,
as Achilles grew up, and his beauty became
the boast of all Thessaly, his mother
would remember the words of the god.
But one day, old men brought tidings,
and said Achilles had been slain at Troy.
And Thetis rent her purple garments,

1. Adapted from the Benjamin Jowett translation.

and tore off her bracelets and her rings
and cast them to the ground. And amid
her pain and her grief she remembered,
and asked, what was wise Apollo doing,
where was the poet who makes such fine
speeches over dinner, where was the seer when
they murdered her child in the first bloom of youth?
And the old men answered her in turn
that Apollo had himself gone down to Troy
and together with the Trojans slew her son.

GROWING STRONG IN SPIRIT

He who would grow strong in spirit
must free himself of reverence and submission.
Of existing laws he will keep a few, but mostly
he will violate both law and custom, and renounce
inadequate conventions of right and wrong.
He will have much to learn from pleasure.
He will not shy away from the destructive act.
Half the house must come down. Only by such means
will he advance virtuously into knowledge.

THE RETINUE OF DIONYSUS

Damon the craftsman (the best there is
in all the Peloponnese) applies
the finishing touches to his Retinue
of Dionysus, in Parian marble.
The god himself in front, divine
splendor and strength in his stride.
Next comes License, and at his side
Intoxication pours the Satyrs' wine
from the amphora with its ivy crown.
Close by, all softness, comes sleep-
inducing Sweetwine, eyes half shut.
And further back the songsters Molpus
and sweet Melus, and Comus, who keeps
the exalted torch of the procession
from going out; and modest Ceremony.
On these things Damon works away.
And while he does, from time to time
he contemplates the money it will bring
— three talents, no paltry sum — from the King
of Syracuse. When to this he adds
his savings, he'll thenceforth lead the life
of a gentleman of means. Then he too
can take up politics — oh joy! — and stand
in the Assembly, and address the Agora.

[Philosophical Scrutiny]

After the already settled Emendatory Work, a philosophical scrutiny of my poems should be made.

Flagrant inconsistencies, illogical possibilities, ridiculous exaggeration should certainly be corrected in the poems, and where the corrections cannot be made the poems should be sacrificed, retaining only any verses of such sacrificed poems as might prove useful later on in the making of new work.

Still the spirit in which the Scrutiny is to be conducted should not be too fanatical.

The profit of personal experience is undoubtedly a sound one; but were it strictly observed it would limit tremendously literary production and even philosophical production. If one ought to wait for old age to risk a word about it, if one ought to wait for the experience of a violent disease in order to mention it, if one ought to experience every sorrow or perturbed state of mind in order to speak of it — one would find that what is left to write of is very little, and indeed many things might not be written at all about as the person who experienced them might not be the person talented to analyse and express them.

Guess work therefore is not to be avoided by any means in a wholesale manner; but of course it must be used cautiously. Guess work indeed — when intelligently directed — loses much of its riskiness, if the user transforms it into a sort of hypothetical experience. This is easier in the description of a battle, of a state of society, of a scenery. By the imagination (and by the help of incidents experienced and remotely or nearly connected) the user can transport himself into the midst of the circumstances and can thus create an experience. The same remark holds good — though it presents more difficulty — in matters of feeling.

I should remark that all philosophers necessarily work largely on guess work — guess work illustrated and elaborated by careful thought and weighing of causes and effects, and by inference, I mean knowledge of other reliable experience.

Moreover the poet in writing of states of mind can also have this sort of experience furnished by his knowledge of himself and has therefore very reliable gauging of what he would feel if he were placed in the imagined conditions.

Also care should be taken not to lose from sight that a state of feeling is true and false, possible and impossible at the same time, or rather by turns. And the poet — who, even when he works the most philosophically, remains an artist — gives one side: which does not mean that he denies the other, or even — though perhaps this is stretching the point — that he wishes to imply that the side he treats is the truest, or the one oftener true. He merely describes a possible and an occurring state of feeling — sometimes very transient, sometimes of some duration.

Very often the poet's work has but a vague meaning: it is a suggestion: the thoughts are to be enlarged by future generations or by his immediate readers: Plato said that poets utter great meanings without realising them themselves.

I have said above that the poet always remains an artist. As an artist he should avoid — without denying — the seemingly highest — seemingly, for it is not quite proven that it is the highest — philosophy of the absolute worthlessness of effort and of the inherent contradiction in every human utterance. If he deny it: he must work. If he accept it: he must work still, though with the consciousness of his work being but finally toys, — at best toys capable of being utilised for some worthier or better purpose, or toys the handling of which prepares for some worthier or better work.

Moreover let us consider the vanity of human things, for this is a clearer way of expressing what I have called "the worthlessness of effort and the inherent contradiction in every human utterance." For few natures, for very few, is it possible to — after accepting it — act accordingly, that is refrain from every action except as subsistence demands. The majority must act; and though producing vain things their impulse to act and their obedience to it are not vain, because it is a following of nature, or of *their* nature. Their actions produce works, which can be divided into two categories, works of immediate utility and works of beauty. The poet does the latter. As human nature has got a craving for beauty manifested in different forms — love, order in his surroundings, scenery, — he purveys to a need. Some work done in vain and the shortness of human life may declare all this vain; but seeing that we do not know the connection between the after life and this life, perhaps even this may be contested. But the mistake lies chiefly in this individualization. The work is not vain when we leave the individual and we consider the result. Here there is no death, at least no sure death: the result may perhaps be immense; there is no shortness of life, but an immense duration of it. So the absolute vanity disappears: at best only a comparative vanity may remain for the individual, but when the individual separates himself from his work and considers only the pleasure or the profit it has given him for a few years and then its vast importance for centuries and centuries even this comparative vanity disappears or vastly lessens.

◆ ◆ ◆

My method of procedure for this Philosophical Scrutiny may be either by taking up the poems one by one and settling them at once, — following the lists and ticking each on the list as it is finished, or effacing it if vowed to destruction; or by considering them first attentively, reporting on them, making a batch of the reports, and afterwards working at them on the basis and in the sequence of the batch: that is the method of procedure of the Emendatory Work.

It may also very well happen that the guess work or rather the intelligent insight into the feelings of others may result in the delineating of more interesting intellectual facts or conditions, than the mere relating of the personal experience of one individual. Moreover — though this is a delicate matter — is not such study of others and penetration of others part of what I call "personal experience"? Does not this penetration — successful or not — influence the individual thought and create states of mind?

Besides, one lives, one hears, and one understands; and the poems one writes, though not true to one's actual life, are true to other lives ("Their First Light," "Walls," "Windows," "Thermopylae") — not generally of course, but specifically — and the reader to whose life the poem fits admires and feels the poem: which is proved by Xenopoulos' liking ("Walls," "Candles") and Pap.'s

("Candles") and Tsocopoulos' ("Sweet Voices").[2] And when one lives, hears, and searches intelligently and tries to write wisely, his work is bound, one may say, to fit some life.

Perhaps Shakespeare had never been jealous in his life, so he ought not to have written *Othello*; perhaps he was never seriously melancholy, so he ought not to have written *Hamlet*; he never murdered, so he ought not to have written *Macbeth*!!!

On Sunday (16 August 1903) I wrote some lines beginning "When a certain day comes, or an hour." I was absolutely sincere at the time. In fact the lines as they now stand are not good, because they have not been worked: it was throwing on paper an impression. In the evening of the very same day I was ill, and the lines seemed to me flat. Yet they *were* sincere: they had the necessary truthfulness for art. So is every sincerity to be laid aside, on account of the short duration of the feeling which prompts its expression? But then art is at a standstill; and speech is condemned — because what is always lasting? And things cannot and should not be lasting, for man would then be "all of a piece" and stagnate in sentimental inactivity, in want of change.

If a thought has really been true for a day, its becoming false the next day does not deprive it of its claim to verity. It may have been only a passing or a short lived truth, but if intelligent and serious it is worthy to be received, both artistically and philosophically.

◆ ◆ ◆

2. The poem titles are all given in Greek. "Sweet Voices" was rewritten and published in 1904 as "Voices."

Here is another example. No poems were sincerer than the "2 M[onth]s"[3] written during and immediately after the great cr[isis] of lib[idinousness?] succeeding on my departure from Athens. Now, say that in time Ale[xis] Mav[roudis][4] comes to be indifferent to me, like Sul. (I was very much in love with him before my departure for Athens), or Bra.; will the poems — so true when they were made — become false? Certainly, certainly not. They will remain true in the past, and, though not applicable any more in my life, seeing that they may remind of a day and perhaps different impression, they will be applicable to feelings of other lives.

The same therefore must apply to other works — really felt at the time. If even for one day, or one hour I felt like the man within "Walls", or like the man of "Windows" the poem is based on a truth, a short-lived truth, but which, for the very reason of its having once existed, may repeat itself in another life, perhaps with as short duration, perhaps with longer. If "Thermopylae" fits but one life, it is true; and it may, indeed the probabilities are that it must.

[Athens and Egypt, 1903]

~ The essay is written in English.

---

3. The poems were "September 1903" and "December 1903." "According to a note by Cavafy, this poem and the one that follows it 'were really written in October and December 1903, but were perfected and catalogued in January 1904.'" Edmund Keeley and George Savidis, eds. and trans., *Passions and Ancient Days* (New York: Dial Press, 1971), 63.

4. Athenian poet and young man of letters whom Cavafy met during his 1903 trip to Greece and "who later settled in Paris and wrote in French under the name Alex. Madis." Lena Savidis, *Cavafy Album: 1863–1910* (Athens: Hermes, 1983), 271.

A CRAFTER OF WINEBOWLS

Upon this winebowl of unmixed silver
made for the house of Heraclides,
wherein impeccable taste prevails —
note the wildflowers, artfully rendered,
the small rivulets, the clusters of thyme,
and there in the middle I placed a youth,
naked, erotic, with one foot trailing
in the water. . . .
                        O Memory, it was you
and your expert assistance I sought
when I gave him the face of someone
that I once loved. No easy thing:
fifteen years have come and gone
since he fell in the defeat at Magnesium.

[On Literary Failure]

Yesterday I vaguely considered, it crossed my thoughts, the possibility of literary failure, & I felt suddenly as if all charm would have left my life, I felt an acute pang at the very idea. I at once imagined my having the enjoyment of love — as I understand & want it — & even this seemed — & very clearly seemed — as if it would not have been sufficient to console me of this great deception.

This proves the verity of "Satrapy."*

11.29.03

~ Except for the poem title, this note is written in English.

*Elsewhere Cavafy records having written this poem in July 1905.

1904

SEPTEMBER 1903

At least let me lose myself now in delusions,
and not feel the emptiness of my life.

But I was so close, so many times —
and yet I froze, and lost my nerve.
Why did my lips stay sealed
while within me wept my empty life,
and my desires wore black in mourning?

To have been so close, so many times
to those eyes, those sensual lips,
to the body I love and dream about.
To have been so close, so many times.

DECEMBER 1903

And if I can't speak of my love,
if I say nothing about your lips, your hair, your eyes —
still your face that I keep in my soul,
your voice that echoes in memory,
the days of September that dawn in dream
color my words and give shape to my sentences,
whatever ideas I take up, whatever my theme.

JANUARY 1904

Ah nights of January,
when I sit and recreate in my thoughts
those moments, and I meet you there,
and hear the last things we said, and the first.

Desperate nights of January,
when the vision fades — and I am alone.
How hurriedly it fades and disappears; gone
the houses, the streets, the lights, the trees;
the erotic image of your body flickers and is gone.

[Craving]

I distinctly felt 1 evening in January 1904 that I should have felt more at ease, with a fuller life, had I to remember a satisfactory morning or day to my craving for a f[uck]; which is proof to the verity of "An Old Man."*

[1904?]

~ Except for the poem title, this note is written in English.

*A poem published in 1897.

OROPHERNES

This handsome face upon the silver coin,
the delicate face that looks as if it smiled —
it is the portraiture of Orophernes
who was the son of Ariarathes.

While he was yet in childhood they expelled him
from Cappadocia, from the ancestral palace,
and sent him to Ionia, to grow up
and be forgotten in the midst of strangers.

Ah, those voluptuous Ionian nights
when, fearlessly, with true Hellenic spirit,
he tasted pleasure to the full extent!
Though always, in his heart, an Asiatic,
he hellenized in manners and in speech —
habitually wore Hellenic dress,
in contrast with his turquoise ornaments;
perfumed himself with perfume of the jasmine;
and among beautiful Ionian youths
was the most beautiful, the most ideal.

Afterward — when the Syrians had prevailed
in Cappadocia, and had crowned him King,
he pounced upon the Kingship that he might
day after day possess a novel joy;
that he might grab the silver and the gold
and at the sight of them exult, and boast
of his great hoard of glittering opulence.
As for the country and the ruling of it —
he never even knew what was going on.

The Cappadocians promptly turned him out;
and in the palace of Demetrius,
in Syria, he sank into a life
of dissipation and of idleness.

One day, however, unusual thoughts assailed
and disconcerted his deep indolence;
he recollected that by reason of
the lineage of Antiochis, his mother —
back to that ancient lady Stratonice —
he was an offshoot of the Syrian crown,
and almost one of the Seleucidae.
And for a little while he roused himself
from his debauchery and drunkenness,
and, all incapable and half bemused,
tried one way or another to intrigue,
tried to do something — to devise a plan,
and failed pitiably and was brought low.

The story of his end must have been told
in writing and the writing have been lost;
or it may be that history passed it by,
being loath — and rightly so — to blot the page
with narrative of no significance.

He who has left after him upon this coin,
some grace of his in juvenescent days,
some gleam of his poetic loveliness,
this feeling memory of an Ionian boy,
was Orophernes, son of Ariarathes.

Translated by John Cavafy

[On Wickedness]

When you feel that you are wicked & it pains you & you have qualms of conscience you are, in reality, wicked no more because you dislike your actions & they no longer belong to you. But when you are wicked with no qualms of conscience & you rather enjoy, then you are wicked unconsciously, so are not wicked at all, for you are not responsible. Then there exists no wickedness after all?

[1904?]

~ This note is written in English.

[The (So-Called) Wicked Man]

The (so-called) wicked man hates badness as much as the (so-called) good man. Only his appreciation of what is bad is different. He explains his actions to himself & does not consider them bad. At the same time that he is committing a very bad action — a crime — there are many things which he disapproves and would not do because he considers that they are bad. So, from one point of view, no "bad man" exists. We are — variously — all, and all want to be, good.

[1905?]*

~ This note is written in English.

*Although the editor of the Greek edition tentatively dates this to 1905, I have relocated it here for thematic reasons.

ON THE STAIRS

As I came down the disreputable stairs, you
were just coming in the door, and for a moment
I saw your unfamiliar face, and you saw me.
Then I turned away, hiding myself,
and you hurried past with your face averted,
and disappeared into that disreputable house
where you'd no more find pleasure than had I.

And yet the love you wanted, I had to give,
and the love I wanted — I could tell
by your restless, weary eyes — you had for me.
Our bodies sensed each other, and sought each other.
Our blood and our flesh understood.
But, shaken, we both of us turned away.

AT THE THEATER

I grew bored watching the stage
so I raised my eyes to the boxes.
And in one of the boxes I saw you
with your enigmatic beauty,
your corrupted youth — and immediately
the things I'd heard about you
earlier that evening came back to me,
and my thoughts and my body were stirred.
And as my eyes fed on your wan beauty,
your weary youth, your very particular clothing,
I imagined you and pictured you
as I'd heard about you that afternoon.

IN THE ENTRANCE TO THE CAFÉ

Something I heard them say next to me
drew my attention to the café entrance,
and there I saw that exquisite body, which looked
as if Love himself had fashioned it
in the fullness of his experience: joyfully
proportioning the limbs, and raising
the statuesque frame; with tenderness
shaping the features of the face —
leaving around the eyes, the brow,
the mouth, a trace of his hands' touch.

DEMARATUS

This is how the young sophist
sketched out the theme — the Character
of Demaratus — which Porphyrius
had suggested in conversation.
(He would work it up rhetorically later.)

Courtier first to King Darius,
then to King Xerxes, and now
accompanying Xerxes and his army —
Demaratus would at last be vindicated.

He had been basely mistreated.
He *was* the son of Ariston, but his enemies
had shamelessly bribed the oracle.
And it wasn't enough just to rob him
of the throne, but when he finally gave in
and resigned himself to living as a private citizen,
they had to insult him before the people,
they had to publicly humiliate him at the festival.

And so he serves King Xerxes with utmost zeal
and presently, with the Persian juggernaut,
makes his way home to Sparta; and once
he's back on the throne, how he'll relish
kicking out that chancer, Leotychides,
how he'll love making him grovel!

And his days are full of care,
as he counsels the Persians, and explains
what they must do to conquer Greece.

So many thoughts, so many worries,
no wonder the days go by so slowly.
So many thoughts, so many worries,
no wonder Demaratus feels no joy;
because it surely isn't joy he feels
(it can't be joy — how could it be —
his misery has never been so great)
when events make it clear
that the Greeks will come out on top.

DESIRES

Like lovely corpses untouched
by age, sealed amid weeping
in splendid tombs, with jasmine
at the feet, and roses at the head —
such are desires that have gone
unfulfilled, that have never known
a single night of pleasure,
or one of its light-flooded dawns.

[Flaws in Great Poems]

It takes time for the flaws in great poems to show. The initial feeling these poems inspire on being published is one of admiration, and until the admiration passes or changes into something else, even the most discerning critics are unable to detect their flaws. This must be due to the curious nature of man, who is able to judge only so long as he does not admire.

[1904?]

[On Monks and Vision]

Monks see things the rest of us don't; they see visions from the supernatural world. They refine their spirit through solitude and reflection and restraint. We blunt ours through social contact, lack of reflection, and indulgence. And so they perceive things we ourselves are unable to. When someone is alone in a quiet room he can easily hear the clock ticking. If others enter, however, with the usual chatter and commotion, he no longer hears it. But the ticking is still there to be heard.

[1904?]

1905

MANUEL KOMNENOS

One melancholy day in September,
his Lordship Emperor Manuel Komnenos
felt death near. The court astrologers
(well paid, of course) prattled away
about how many years he still had left.
But while they talked on, the Emperor,
remembering pious customs of yore,
commands that from the monastic cells
ecclesiastical vestments be brought,
and he puts them on, and rejoices to present
the unassuming mien of a priest or a monk.

Happy are they who believe,
and like Lord Emperor Manuel end their days
modestly dressed in their faith.

I WENT

I was not bound. I let go
completely, and went — plunged
through the luminous night, to delights
half real, half spun in my brain.
And I drank of heady wine,
such as the lords of pleasure drink.

[Mistress of the World]

A young poet came to see me. He was extremely poor, living from his literary labors, and it seemed a little as if it distressed him, seeing the nice house I live in, the servant bringing the elegant tea-tray, my clothes from the house of a good tailor. He said: "It's terrible having to struggle to make ends meet, running after subscribers for your magazine, buyers for your book."

I didn't want to leave him in his error, so I said a few things to him, more or less as follows. His situation was indeed an unpleasant and difficult one — but how much my small luxuries have cost me! For their sake I'd abandoned my true path to become a civil servant (how ridiculous) and now how many precious hours I spend — and lose — each day (to which must be added the hours of fatigue and stupefaction that follow). What a loss, what a loss — what a betrayal. While he, poor though he is, never loses a moment on such things. He's always there, a faithful and dutiful child of Art.

How often, in the middle of work, a wonderful idea comes to me, some rare image, sudden verses rising as if fully formed, and I have to put them aside, because the service can't wait. Then when I go home, and have revived somewhat, I try to call them up again — and they're gone. And so it should be. It's as if Art were telling me: "I am not your servant, to be dismissed when I come, and to come when it pleases you. I am the supreme Mistress of the world. And if you've turned your back on me — poor wretch and traitor that you are — for your pathetic little home, your pathetic fancy clothes, your pathetic social standing — then be content with them (but how could you be?) and with those few moments when I come and you happen to be ready, waiting to receive me on your doorstep — as you should be, every day."

June 1905

IONIC

That we smashed their statues
and drove them from their temples
doesn't at all mean the gods have died.
Land of Ionia — they love you still,
in their souls they still remember.
When light of an August morning kindles above you,
some power from their lives
quickens your atmosphere,
and sometimes, the figure of a youth
— ethereal, indefinite —
swiftly makes its way above your hills.

THE SATRAPY

What a disaster, whilst you are made for beautiful and great acts, this iniquitous fate of yours ever to refuse you encouragement and success; always do littlenesses and base customs, and indifferences stand in your way. And how terrible the day on which you yield (the day on which you abandon yourself, and yield), and you leave, a wayfarer for Susa, and you go to the monarch Artaxerxes who admits you with favour in his court, and offers you satrapies, and the like. And you, you accept these things in despair; these things which you do not desire. Other things does your soul demand, for other things is your soul weeping — the praise of the Demos and of the Sophists; the difficult and invaluable "Euges";* the Agora,** the theatre, the crowns of laurel. These things Artaxerxes cannot give you; these things you will not find in the satrapy; and what sort of life will be yours without them.

Translated by C. P. Cavafy

* Euges — exclamations of approval

** Agora — forum

[No Small Thing]

Like a good tailor who makes a suit of clothing that looks splendid on one person (or possibly two) or an overcoat that is right for two or three — just so my poems can be applied — made "to fit"* — a single case (possibly two, three). The comparison is (on the surface only) somewhat demeaning; but, I believe, it is nevertheless apt and reassuring. If my poems lack general applicability, they at least possess a partial one. That is no small thing. Their verity is thereby guaranteed.

7.9.05

* In English in the original.

AS BEST YOU CAN

And if you cannot make your life
the way you want it — do this, at least,
as best you can: don't cheapen it
in the web of worldly relations,
the constant motion and incessant talk.

Don't cheapen it by parading it,
by dragging it around and exposing it
to the everyday inanity
of social engagements and soirées,
until it's no better than some tiring hanger-on.

[The New Phase of Love]

What makes English literature cold for me — aside from certain shortcomings of the English language — is its — how shall I put it — conservative nature — its inability, or unwillingness — to depart from the well-trod path, and its fear of coming into conflict with morality — with pseudo-morality, for how else characterize a morality that pretends ignorance?

Over the past ten years, how many French books — both good and bad — have been written that examine and bravely take into account the new phase of love. It is not new, of course; it has merely been ignored for centuries, in the superstitious belief that it was a form of madness (science says otherwise) or something criminal (reason says otherwise). Yet not a single book in English, that I know of. Why? For fear of coming into conflict with prejudice. Nevertheless, this form of love exists even among the English, just as it exists, and has existed, in all societies, though to be sure never in great numbers.

October 1905

HE SWEARS

Every so often he swears
                that he'll start a better life.
But when night comes on
                with its own advice,
with its many promises
                and its compromises,
but when night comes on
                with all the force of
a body that wants and
                demands — once again
he abandons himself to the old fatal joy.

[An Object of Speculation]

The miserable laws of society — having nothing to do with health, nor the result of reasoned judgment — have diminished my work. They've hobbled my means of expression, hindered my ability to move and enlighten others who are made like me. The difficult circumstances of my life forced me to go to great lengths to become fluent in the English language. A real pity. If I had taken — if circumstances had permitted it, if French had been as useful to me — the same pains with French, perhaps by using it — with things made easier for me by its pronouns, which both declare and conceal — I would have been able to express myself with greater freedom. So, what am I to do? Artistically, I never had a chance. And I shall go on being an object of speculation; and shall be understood most fully by what I have disavowed.

12.15.05

1906

[On Art and Sincerity]

What a deceitful thing Art is when you want to impose sincerity. You sit down and write — often by guess work — about experiences, then as time goes by you begin to wonder whether you weren't misled. I wrote "Candles," "The Souls of Old Men," and "An Old Man" about old age. Approaching old age — or middle age — I've realized that the last of these poems does not give an accurate account of it. I still consider "The Souls of Old Men" to be accurate. But when I reach 70, perhaps I'll find that it too is false. "Candles," I hope, is safe.

Descriptive poetry — historical events, the photo-depiction (hideous word!) of nature — may be safe. But it is a small and somehow short-lived sort of thing.

1906

IDES OF MARCH

Fear greatness, O my soul.
Learn to master your ambitions;
and if you cannot, then pursue them
with hesitation and great caution.
And the more you get ahead, so much the more
should you be circumspect and wary.

And when you reach your zenith, Caesar at last;
when you've assumed the shape
of a famous man — then above all
look about you as you step into the street
with your retinue, a man of prominence and power,
and if one should approach you from the crowd,
an Artemidorus bearing a letter —
his words tumbling out, "Read this
instantly . . . of great importance" —
don't fail to stop; don't fail to postpone
your meetings and assorted tasks.
Push past the throngs who hail you
and would kiss your hand (you can see them later) —
let even the Senate wait, if it must;
and acquaint yourself without delay
with the grave tidings of Artemidorus.

PHILHELLENE

See that the engraving be skillfully done,
that the expression be one of solemn majesty.
Make the diadem on the slender side;
the wide Parthian ones aren't to my taste.
The inscription, as usual, in Greek;
nothing excessive, nothing pompous,
lest that busybody the proconsul
take it wrong and report back to Rome;
yet nor should it be stinting in its praise.
And on the reverse, something choice —
a discus thrower perhaps: young, handsome.
Above all, I urge you, see to it
(by the gods, Sispathis, don't forget!)
that after "King" and "Savior," in elegant letters,
"Philhellene" — lover of the Greeks — be inscribed.
And don't start in with your "Greeks, what Greeks?"
and "Where's anything Greek, out here
beyond Phraata, on the far side of Zagros?"
Since so many others more barbarian than us
write it, so shall we. And remember, too
that occasionally sophists, and versifiers,
and others of that ilk, come to us here from Syria.
So I wouldn't say that we are un-Hellenic.

POSEIDONIANS

The people of Poseidonia who dwell in the Tyrrhenian Gulf though they were originally Greeks, have become completely barbarised, becoming Tyrrhenians or Romans, and have changed their language, and all the rest of their national habits. But one Greek festival they do celebrate even to the present day, in which they meet and recollect their ancient names and customs, and bewail their loss to one another, and then, when they have wept for them, they go home.

Athenaeus[5]

After so many centuries of intermingling
with Romans and Tyrrhenians and other foreign races,
the Poseidonians had forgotten their Greek.
All that remained to them of their heritage
was a charming Greek festival, with flutes and lyres,
with athletic events and laurel wreaths.
And as the festival drew to a close,
it was the custom to tell of the old ways,
and speak the old Greek names,
which few now could understand.
And so the festival always ended
on a melancholy note, for the Poseidonians
remembered they too had once been Greek
— Greeks of Magna Gaecia —
and now look how they had fallen,
how they'd taken up barbarian ways
and spoke a barbarian tongue,
by Hellenism — oh disaster! — cast aside.

5. Adapted from the translation by Charles Duke Yonge (1854).

[From a Draft of a Letter to Marika Tsaliki]

Alexandria
9 September 1906

My dear Marika,

I received your letter of August 27, and was very happy to learn your news. Paul and I are fine; and as for the heat we have nothing to complain of this year — it was very mild.

Last Monday (September 3) John arrived; and the change appeared to have done him much good. He stayed with us for three days, and then went to Cairo. To be sure, after Prinkipo and Europe, he will not find the climate there especially pleasant. But patience — in six weeks' time the good weather will begin.

Thank you so much for sending the invitation to the Photiadis-Papas wedding. (I know Dr. Photiadis from his wise and valuable book The Language Question and Our Educational Renaissance.) The invitation is indeed of great interest. "*Kat'eme*" is perfectly fine. It would be foolish to think that we must keep the living language locked away only in books, as if in a palace or in prison. It must bravely step forth and partake in all of life's relations. To be sure, it is unfortunate that this living Greek language is not the same for all demoticists. But this misfortune was not to be avoided. In the beginning — 20 years ago — a shared rebellion against Katharevousa,* a shared effort united the demoticists, and the differences between their systems and between their creative leanings (for those who were artists), though latent, remained hidden and did not serve to divide. In time, however, as the demotic movement gained momentum, the demoticists began to splinter into groups, and differing attitudes towards language emerged, sometimes accompanied, for certain

* "Katharevousa" — Purist Greek

zealots, by considerable passion. This was natural given the effect of Katharevousa on the spoken language. Some — myself among them — balked at sacrificing Katharevousa wholesale, and are not content to condemn the linguistic labors of a century (and more than a century); we are happy to admit not only words from antiquity (in their true shape), but also grammatical forms, when these words and forms occur or have passed into urban speech, or when they help to enrich and beautify the language. This is not to say that it would not have been better if from the start the language, restricted to its natural morphology, had developed more simply and with greater regularity. But the departure from demotic began many generations ago; those of us who now return to the language do so as religious pilgrims — pilgrims filled with reverence and emotion who, upon entering the shrine, shall of course remove all the tasteless embellishments and needless finery that disfigure it, but this without violence and without prejudice, lest we overlook and throw onto the heap —imbeciles that we are — some lekythos* of gold, or some coffer in mother-of-pearl.

* "lekythos" — an ancient Greek oil flask

[On Postponing to Publish]

By my postponing, & repostponing to publish, what a gain I have had! Think of "Songs," of "Ischean Inspiration," of trash (at the age of 25, 26, & 27 & 28) of Byzantine poems, of "Conception of Beauty," of "Harem," of "The Mistress Sleeps," of "Prosody," of "The Beauty of Evil," of "When, friends, I was in love . . . ," of "Systems" (Magi, Philosophers etc. speaking rot), of "Cleopatra," of "Porphyrius," of "Lament" (with the stupid voices of Wife, Parents, Child etc.) & many others which would disgrace me now.

What a gain!

10.1.06

And all those poems written between 19 and 22. What wretched trash!

~ Except for one of the poem titles ("Harem"), this note is written in English.

1907

[On Self-Interest]

Sometimes when I am thinking, and coming to grips with difficult concepts and interconnections, and their consequences, and an idea comes to me that others aren't in a position to think through or to grasp as I do; this makes me "uncomfortable."* Because it immediately occurs to me: How unfair, that I with my genius am neither well known nor rewarded. And at the next moment I feel relief in the idea that I may be deceived, and that there may be many others filled with thoughts just as profound and penetrating. How fine a thing, then, is Self-Interest, or the Pursuit of Reward! I take greater comfort at the thought that I am one among many, than that I am superior, and deprived of my just reward.

1.3.07

* In English in the original.

[On Fervor]

Without fervor — and here I also include anger — mankind is unable to work. When in its grip, however, he doesn't work especially well. The fervor must pass before he can really accomplish anything, but even then — in a collected state — the things he creates have their origin in that period of fervor. Someone with too much of it does inferior work; likewise someone with none at all.

1.24.07

[On Alexandria]

I've grown used to Alexandria by now, and probably even if I were wealthy I'd go on living here. Even so, how it oppresses me. What a hardship, what a burden a small city is. What a curb on one's freedom.

I'd go on living here (then again, I'm not altogether certain that I would) because it's like a homeland to me, because it's all bound up with my life's memories.

But how much someone like me — different as I am — needs a big city.

London, for instance. Ever since . . . P. M. left, I haven't stopped thinking about it.

4.28.07

[Second Occupations]

A second occupation — anything done to gain a livelihood — though of course nothing so strenuous or time-consuming as to take up all of his day — is a great asset for the artist. It *refreshes him,** rids him of his vapors, restores him almost. This is true for some artists at least.

5.13.07

* In English in the original.

MARC ANTONY DYING

But when he heard the women weeping,
and lamenting what had become of him —
Cleopatra with her oriental gestures,
the slaves with their barbarized Greek —
all the pride within him
reared up, his Italian blood recoiled,
and everything he'd worshiped blindly up till then,
his riotous Alexandrian life,
appeared alien to him, of no interest.
And he said: "Let them not weep for him,
rather they should sing his praise
as one who achieved the heights of power,
and amassed great wealth.
And if now he had fallen, it wasn't ignobly,
but as a Roman by a Roman overcome."

ONE NIGHT

It was a crude, shabby room
hidden away over a dubious tavern.
From the window you could see the lane,
narrow and squalid. From downstairs
came the voices of local workmen,
playing cards and carrying on.

And there, on that humble, lowly bed,
I had love's body, I tasted the red
voluptuous lips of drunkenness,
the red of such drunkenness that
even now, writing after so many years,
alone in my house, I am drunk again.

THE TOBACCONIST'S WINDOW

They stood in a throng of people
near the bright window of a tobacconist.
By chance their eyes met,
and timidly, uncertainly,
they communicated their desires,
the unlawful desires of their flesh.
A few uneasy steps down the street —
and then the smile, the hint of a nod.

And at last, the closed carriage, the sensuous
coming together of bodies, the hands
entwining, lips pressing together.

[A Limited Circle of Pleasure]

I was reading tonight about Baudelaire. And the author of the book I was reading seemed as if he were *épaté* by "Fleurs du Mal." I haven't reread "Fleurs du Mal" in some time. From what I remember, it is not so terribly *épatant.* And it seems to me that Baudelaire was confined to a very limited circle of pleasure. Take last night; or Wednesday past; and how many other times that I have experienced, and carried out, and imagined, and silently orchestrated more unusual forms of gratification.

9.22.07

INDEPENDENCE

In three recent issues of *Panathenaia*, much has been written about how little reading Greeks do, and how little encouragement is given to the book and the periodical. All opinions concurred that literature does not receive the support it should when it comes to the author's material well-being, and the public's moral well-being.

That this situation is disagreeable and injurious is beyond dispute. The lack of suitable material support has impeded the development of many talents (if not talents of the first order, since genius, I believe, will get its work done with or without encouragement), but worthy talents nonetheless, both in their own right, and in terms of their role in the shaping of literature as a whole.

But alongside so much that is disagreeable and injurious in this situation — and its effects become more palpable by the day — we should also note, by way of consolation, one benefit: namely, the intellectual independence it bestows on us.

When an author knows that, at all events, only a few copies of a particular printing are going to sell, and that his book is destined to circulate primarily through lending libraries, a number of hindrances instantly fall away, and he acquires immense freedom in his creative endeavor.

An author conscious of the certainty, or even the possibility, of his book's print-run selling out, and perhaps later editions as well, this author is now and again influenced by these future sales. However sincere he may be, however sure of himself, there will be moments — almost without his wishing it, or his being aware of it — when, knowing what the public thinks, and what it likes, and what it buys, he will make small sacrifices: he will phrase this bit a little differently, or he will leave that part out. And there is nothing more disastrous for Art (I cringe to think of it) than to put this bit a little differently, or to leave that part out.

To this independence I attribute a large part of the qualitative progress of contemporary Greek letters.

Let me further say that, while the indifference shown to our letters by the Greek public is undeniably painful, and while a comparison with other nations — where reading is considered a virtual duty — does not favor us, still we should not forget that even elsewhere the most elevated examples of poetic expression, or the most finely-tuned prose, do not always — at least on their first appearance — find a large audience.

[Fall 1907?]

1908

27 JUNE 1906, 2 P.M.

When the Christians brought out the innocent
seventeen-year-old boy for hanging,
his mother, who'd been crawling in the dust
close by the gallows, and tearing at her hair
in the brutal, midday sun, began shrieking
and howling like a wild animal, and then,
worn down by grief, broke into lament:
"My son, only seventeen years you lived for me. . . ."
And when they led him up the steps of the gallows
and slipped the noose around his neck,
and hanged the innocent seventeen-year-old boy,
and as he dangled pitifully over the abyss,
as his young, well-molded body twitched
in its final agony, his martyred mother,
writhing in the dust, did not speak of years now:
"Seventeen days only," she keened,
"Seventeen days only I had you for my delight. . . ."

HIDDEN THINGS

From all that I've said and all I have done,
don't seek to find out who I was.
Certain impediments stood in the way,
transforming my actions and my manner of life.
Certain impediments stood in the way,
and often checked me on the verge of speech.
In my least noticed acts, in the most veiled
of my writings — only there will you understand me.
But maybe, in the end, it isn't worth
so much thought and effort to find me out.
Later, in a more perfect society,
someone made like me
is sure to come forward and act freely.

[The Beauty of the Poorer Classes]

The beauty of the poorer classes, of young men struggling to get by, pleases me, and moves me. Servants, laborers, petty commercial clerks and shop assistants. Their beauty is, one supposes, a recompense for their deprivations. Long hours and constant activity keep their bodies fit. They are almost always on the lean side. Their faces — pale when they work in shops, sunburnt when out of doors — possess an attractive, a poetic color. This is in contrast to the children of the well-to-do, who are either sickly, and foul of body, or fleshy and grease-stained from their gluttony, and their drinking, and their featherbeds. As if in their bloated or their shrunken faces you could see all the ugliness of the theft and robbery of their inheritances and the interest thereon.

6.29.08

[Fresh on the Impression . . .]

Fresh on the impression, or a little after, the poem is made. The impression — sensual or intellectual — was both vivid, and utterly sincere; the poem (not necessarily because the impression was that way; but by happy coincidence) turned out well: itself vivid and sincere. Then time passes. That same impression — either because other, previously unknown circumstances have intervened, or because of new developments vis-à-vis the thing or person that kindled it — now seems hackneyed and trivial. Likewise the poem it generated. Yet I'm not sure if that's how it should be. Why should I take the poem out of the atmosphere of 1904 and put it into the atmosphere of 1908? (Fortunately, the poems are often cryptic; thus other — comparable — feelings or states of mind can easily be made to fit them.)

7.11.08

[On Seriousness]

I know that, in order to succeed in life, and command respect, one must be a serious person. But it's hard for me to be serious, I don't value seriousness.

Let me explain what I mean. I like seriousness only in serious things; that is, 1/2 hour, or one hour, or two or three hours of seriousness a day. Often, to be sure, almost an entire day of it.

Otherwise, I like jokes, drollery, the well-turned irony, *humbugging*.*

But it is simply not practical.

It makes it harder to get things done.

Because for the most part you are dealing with morons and ignoramuses. These sorts of people are always serious. Faces serious as dumb beasts; how do you expect them to joke around, when they don't understand? Their serious faces are an illusion. Everything is a problem and an obstacle to their slow and untutored intelligence. That's why, like oxen or sheep (animals wear utterly serious expressions), their features are so steeped in seriousness.

A humorous person is generally looked down on, or at least not paid much attention; he doesn't inspire a great deal of confidence.

That is why I go out of my way to present a serious mien to most people. I have found that it makes my affairs go much more smoothly. On the inside, I'm forever laughing and joking around.

10.26.08

* In English in the original.

1909

DAYS OF 1903

I never found them again — so quickly lost.
The poetic eyes, the pallid cheeks.
The street at the onset of dusk.

I never found them again — those chance
possessions so easily let go of
and ever since so desperately longed for —
the poetic eyes, the pallid cheeks,
those lips I never found again.

["The Time of Year I Love . . ."]

The time of year I love is summer. The real summer, that is, of Egypt and Greece: the intense sunlight, the triumph of high noon, the spent lassitude of August nights. Still, I can't say that I work (as an artist, I mean) any more in summertime. The shapes and sensations of summer provide me with a wealth of impressions; but I've never noticed that I've jotted them down, or translated them directly into literary form. I say directly, because artistic impressions sometimes go unused for long periods; they produce other thoughts, are reshaped by fresh influences, and when they crystallize into written words, we have difficulty remembering which of those moments was the original cause, the source from which the words truly spring.

[Summer 1909?]

COME BACK

Come back often and take me,
beloved sensation, come and take me
when memory wakes in the body
and old desires run in the vein,
when lips and skin remember
and hands seem to touch again —

Come back often and take me at night
when lips and skin remember.

1910

SELEUCID'S DISPLEASURE

Demetrius the Seleucid wasn't at all pleased
to learn that a Ptolemy had arrived in Italy
in such a sorry state: with no more
than three or four servants; humbly dressed
and on foot. At this rate, they'd be
laughing stocks in no time, their lineage
the butt of Roman jokes. That they had become
little more than servants of the Romans,
Seleucid knew; that it was the Romans
who gave and took away their thrones,
arbitrarily, at a whim, he knew this too.
But in appearance at least let them maintain
some kind of majesty; let them not forget
they were still kings; that even now
they were called — god help them! — kings.

Which is why the Seleucid was so upset;
and straightaway he offered Ptolemy
garments dyed in porphyry, a splendid crown,
costly gems and jewelry, scores of domestics
and retainers, his most expensive horses —
that he might appear in Rome with due decorum,
like the Greek, the Alexandrian monarch he was.

But the Lagid, who had come to beg,
knew his business and refused it all.
He'd no use for such extravagance.
Poorly dressed and humble he entered Rome,
lodging at the home of a simple craftsman.
And later, he presented himself to the Senate
as someone down on his luck, a pauper,
so as to beg with all the more effect.

Demetrius I Soter (185-150 B. C.), son of the Hellenistic ruler Seleucus IV Philopator, spent the first twenty-four years of his life in Rome as a political hostage.

Ptolemy VI Philometor (circa 186-145 B. C.), Hellenistic ruler of Egypt, visited Rome in 164 to ask for backing in his power struggle with his brother.

ACCOMPLISHED FACTS

Sick with fear and suspicion —
our thoughts addled, our eyes wild —
we give way to panic, and think only of
how to avoid this certain danger that looms
so horrifically over us. But no —
we were mistaken. It's not who we thought
there in the road — the reports were wrong,
or we heard them wrong, or misunderstood.
Some other disaster we weren't expecting
sudden, ferocious, unprepared for — who had time? —
steals up on us and sweeps us away.

[On Writing and the Erotic]

My life moves through fluctuations of the sensual, through conceptualizations — realized at times — of the erotic.

My work tends toward thought.

Maybe that's how it should be.

Moreover, my work is like that amphora I spoke of. It permits a variety of interpretations.

And my erotic life *does* get declared — obscure only to the ignorant. Were it declared more extensively, it might not prove sufficient artistic ground to hold me, to sustain me.

I go about it like the ancients. They wrote history, philosophy, mythological dramas of the tragic, driven — so many of them — by desire . . . just like me.

6.20.10

[The New Philosophical Ideas]

How repellent these new philosophical ideas are, the ones preaching ruthlessness, the rightful domination by the strong, the supposed salutary effect of strife, which eliminates the small and the weak, etc., etc. Since we *must* live in society, since that's where civilization comes from, since it is by such means that we managed to withstand the brutal life conditions that confronted mankind at the outset — what's all this wild talk about ruthlessness, domination, etc. Were we really to put these things into practice, we would find that they lead to annihilation. One man of superior strength here will, directly or indirectly, destroy ten weaker ones; another there will do the same to ten more; and so on and so forth. Only the strong will be left. Of these, some will be a little less strong. Once the former weaklings are out of the picture, *they* will be the weak ones, and will also have to be destroyed ten, or five, or two at a time. Until only the strongest one is left, or a few of equal strength. But how will they ever survive that way? Not ruthlessness; but Mercy, Compassion, Tolerance, Kindness (all, of course, in due measure, without excess) constitute Strength as well as wisdom.

9.10.10

ITHACA

When you set out on your way to Ithaca,
pray that your journey be a long one,
full of adventures, full of secret knowledge.
As for Cyclops and the Laistrygonians,
as for angry Poseidon, have no fear:
You will never meet with such as these
if you keep your mind on higher things, if superior
sentiments govern your spirit and your body.
Laistrygonians, Cyclops, angry Poseidon —
you will not meet them along the way
unless you carry them in your soul,
unless your own soul calls them into being.

Pray that your journey be a long one.
and that many's the summer morning
when — with what contentment, what joy —
you enter harbors for the very first time.
Put in at the Phoenician ports-of-call,
and there fill your hold with precious cargo:
mother of pearl and coral, ebony and amber,
and all manner of voluptuous perfumes —
above all, a profusion of voluptuous perfumes.
To the many cities of Egypt pay a visit
to be instructed and enlightened by the learned.

Never let Ithaca slip from your thoughts.
Arriving there is what you set out to do.
But no need to hurry your trip at all.
Better it should last for many years. Better
you be old when at last you make landfall,
rich with all you've gained along the way,
not expecting Ithaca to give you riches.

Ithaca gave you the marvelous journey.
Without it, you would never have set out.
Ithaca has nothing more to give you.

And if you find it poor, Ithaca didn't deceive you.
Wise as you'll be, with all your experience,
you'll have already understood what these Ithacas mean.

THE GOD ABANDONS ANTONY

When suddenly at midnight hour you hear
an invisible band of revelers going past
with exquisite music, with laughter —
don't give in to useless grieving
for your luck that has run out, your efforts
that have failed, your great schemes gone awry.
Like one long prepared, like a man of courage,
say goodbye to her — the Alexandria that is leaving.
Above all, don't lie to yourself, don't say
it was a dream, that your ears deceived you.
Don't stoop to such futile hopes.
Like one long prepared, like a man of courage,
as befits someone worthy of such a city —
go up to the window now and listen
with emotion, but with none of the coward's
pleading and complaining — listen
as a final pleasure to the music, the exquisite
instruments of that mystic company,
and say goodbye to her — the Alexandria you are losing.

1911

THE TOMB OF LYSIAS THE GRAMMARIAN

Immediately to the right, as you enter the library
of Beirut, we buried Lysias, the learned
grammarian. The spot is admirably suited.
We put him close to the things he remembers,
perhaps, even there: texts, grammars, scholia,
variants, volumes of commentary on Greek idioms.
Moreover, he's where we can see his tomb, and pay
our respects, as we pass on through to the books.

[*A* Discipline de Vie]

We labor, virtuously, for future generations. Preparing the way for a *discipline de vie*; laying its foundations; which is perhaps of even greater benefit, since they may enjoy longer lives.

early April, 1911

HEARING OF LOVE

When you hear of passionate love, tremble
and be moved, like an esthète.
But afterwards remember, with contentment,
all the things imagination shaped for you: these
remember first; and then the rest, the lesser things,
tangible and more real, that life has given you
to experience and enjoy.
You had your share of such loves too.

THEODOTUS

If you are one of the truly elect,
take care how you obtain your power.
However exalted you may be, however much
the city-states acclaim your deeds
in Italy and in Thessaly, however many honors
your backers might push through in Rome —
neither your joy, nor sense of triumph will remain,
nor will you feel yourself a superior — superior! —
human being, when in Alexandria
Theodotus brings you, on a bloody platter,
wretched Pompey's head.

And don't be lulled by thinking that your life —
circumscribed, orderly, mundane —
has nothing so horrific or sensational in store.
Perhaps this very hour, through the door
of your neighbor's well-kept house,
steps Theodotus — invisible, impalpable —
bearing just such a ghastly head.

Theodotus of Chios, an adviser to Ptolemy XIII of Egypt.
He is said to have delivered the head of Roman consul Pompey
to the victorious Julius Caesar in 48 B.C.

I HAVE GAZED SO LONG —

I have gazed so long at beauty
that it has come to fill all my vision.

Lines of the body. Red lips. Amorous limbs.
Hair as if copied from Greek statues —
lovely to look at, always, even uncombed
and falling, just slightly, over the white
forehead. Shapes of love, as my poetry
wanted them . . . in the nights of my youth,
encountered, secretly, in my nights . . .

[Visions of Beauty]

— U U —	U U — U
— U U —	U U — U
— U — U	U — U

That was it, more or less. That's how I jotted it down on a cigarette pack the other day, from which I transcribe it here.

When I wrote it down — giving a prosodic rendering of a song that two young men were singing as they passed by — I imagined that I had really done something. I had done nothing. I now see that the tune was nothing out of the ordinary, though their voices were pleasant. But once they drew me to the window, both the melody and the voices took on even greater beauty, because the two youths — boys around 22 or 23 — were themselves visions of beauty.

What bodies, what hair, what faces, what lips! They were there only for a moment, then passed on; and I, the artist, imagined that I had accomplished something by preserving a melody. A melody which I now find unremarkable, and in all probability of no use. The only touch of poetry that went past me that day was the beauty of the two young men. This, if memory preserves any of it, and brings it back to me in a moment of creative emotion, may perhaps leave in my art something of its brief passage the other day.

10.17.11

TO ANTIOCHUS EPIPHANES

Said the Antiochian youth to the King:
"A cherished hope beats in my heart —
Back in the struggle, Antiochus Epiphanes,
the Macedonians back in the battle again.
Oh were they to win I would gladly part with
my lion and my horses, the Pan made of coral,
the elegant palace, the gardens at Tyre,
and all else you gave me Antiochus Epiphanes."

It's possible that the King was a trifle moved;
but then he remembered his father and brother
and he bit his tongue. (Spies might be abroad
who'd repeat what he said.) Besides, unsurprisingly,
soon enough at Pydna came the sickening conclusion.

DANGEROUS PURSUITS

The words of Myrtias (Syrian student
in Alexandria, during the reign of Augustus
Constans and Augustus Constantius;
half pagan, and half Christianized):
"Fortified by study and contemplation,
I will not go in cowardly fear of my passions,
I will give my body entirely to pleasure,
to all the things that I've dreamed about,
to the wildest promptings of my flesh,
the secret urges of my blood — without
the least fear, because I know that
when I set my mind to it — and I *will*,
fortified as I'll be by study and contemplation —
at crucial moments my ascetic spirit
will come back to me, undiminished."

A RARE EXCEPTION

He is an old man. Spent, bent down,
ravaged by the years and bad living,
he slowly makes his way across the street.
But as he turns in at his door, as he shuts
his decrepitude and age from view, he considers
the stake he still has in youth.

Now it's *his* verses the young recite,
his visions that fill their vivid eyes.
Their healthy and sensuous minds
and sturdy, well-molded flesh
are moved by his own articulation of the beautiful.

III. AFTERWORD

THE AESTHETICS OF PLEASURE

According to the meticulous records Cavafy kept of the poems he wrote and revised between the years 1891 and 1925, there is only one year in which he wrote no poems at all: 1902. The same year also saw Cavafy experiment with a new form of writing that he kept up, intermittently, for the next ten years: the short reflections that were printed in Greek, fifty years after his death, as "Unpublished Notes on Poetics and Ethics."[1] If Cavafy's low output in the first two years of the new century (he wrote only one poem, "Thermopylae," in 1901) can be tied to the emotional crisis that had begun in the waning years of the preceding century, then perhaps the Notes can be associated with the poet's gradual emergence from the crisis over the coming few years.[2] If they were begun at an apparent low point in his life, the Notes end at a high point: 1911, a year distinguished by the publication of two of Cavafy's most identifiable poems, "Ithaca" and "The God Abandons Antony," and later chosen by the poet as the year that marked the "before" and "after" of his poetic development.

The most fruitful year in terms of the Notes was the first, 1902: in the second half of that year, Cavafy composed at least seven of them—the largest number for any one year. Clearly the possibilities of this new form stimulated him. Still, they didn't come all in the spurt; if Cavafy's own dating is to be trusted, between July and December of that first year he wrote exactly one a

1. Hereafter, I will refer to these simply as (uppercase) Notes, to distinguish them from the so-called "confessional notes," discussed later.

2. G. P. Savidis, in his study of Cavafy's manuscripts, concludes that "around 1899 Cavafy's poetic conscience undergoes a crisis which it only begins to issue from in 1901." *Cavafy's Editions* (Athens: Ikaros, 1991), 143. He is noncommittal on its causes. G. P. Savidis writes: "Whether this crisis relates to the series of family bereavements that befell the poet during those years, or with his gradual release from his sexual complex, or with the fact that in 1903 Cavafy would be forty years of age, is an issue that cannot absorb us here" (144). Savidis sees the "Philosophical Scrutiny" as marking the terminus of the crisis.

month, except for November, during which he wrote two. This suggests that they were more a matter of discipline than inspiration: an exercise Cavafy set himself as a means of overcoming whatever block kept him from writing any poems between January 1901 and May 1903. (By contrast, Cavafy records having written six poems in 1900.) The subjects of the Notes are various: language, writing, epistemology. By the fall of 1902, however, sexuality emerges as a major theme; over time, it would become a central focus of his verse as well.

There is nothing tentative about these first venturings into the realm of sexuality—of unconventional sexuality—not even in the hesitation that opens the first of these notes: "It crossed my mind tonight to write about my love — but I'm not going to"; for this is quickly followed by the declaration that "I have freed myself from [prejudice]," as opposed to "those still enslaved to it." Likewise the two notes that follow, one dealing with "subservience — while in the act of writing — to a sensation or condition of sexual arousal," the other with sexual deviance as "the root of greatness." Cavafy writes with the confidence of someone who has followed from a distance the discourse on sexuality as it emerged in the later nineteenth century, first in the creative work of the Decadents in France and the Aesthetes in England, and then in the science-minded work of sexologists like Havelock Ellis, whose groundbreaking if problematic study of homosexuality, *Sexual Inversion,* had appeared five years earlier.

The same confident tone is heard—amplified—in an unpublished poem tentatively dated as June of the following year. "Growing Strong in Spirit" (1903) is the most Nietzschean of Cavafy's poems. (Cavafy owned a *Selected Writings* of Nietzsche in French, and appears to have read it with care.)[3] Nor is the Nietzschean spirit far off in the two poems flanking "Growing Strong in Spirit" chronologically: "Perfidy," a poem that raises questions about the reliability of the divine word; and "The Retinue of Dionysus," which lays bare the intersection of art and the will to power, while perhaps commenting ironically on Nietzsche's notion of the Dionysian. "Growing Strong in Spirit" itself reads like a manifesto promoting transgression and creative destruction—"Half

3. "Pages Choisies" in Henri Albert trans., *Oeuvres completes de Frederic Nietzsche* (Paris, 1899). See Michaela Karabini-Iatrou, ed., *Cavafy's Library* (Athens: Ermis, 2003), 102.

the house must come down," it tells us—in the service of both personal revelation (what we'd call "self-realization" today) and, secondarily, societal renewal—this well before the modernist heyday of the manifesto. The boldness of Cavafy's pronouncements in the twelve-month period between July 1902 and July 1903 ("Boldness" is the title of a lost poem from June 1903) laid the groundwork for the poetic breakthroughs of the following two years. The same spirit emboldened Cavafy, in the fall of 1903, to undertake a "philosophical scrutiny" of his poetic output to date, a project articulated in a document that some consider Cavafy's single most significant piece of prose.

Made up of nine pages of densely written shorthand, this untitled manuscript (hereafter "Scrutiny") outlines in English an ambitious attempt to establish sound criteria for judging and weeding out his completed work, based on principles of empiricism, rationality, and common sense:

> Flagrant inconsistencies, illogical possibilities, ridiculous exaggeration should certainly be corrected in the poems, and where the corrections cannot be made the poems should be sacrificed.

If "Growing Strong in Spirit" tackled "inadequate conventions of right and wrong," here Cavafy sets out to eliminate inadequate forms of poetry. If, according to that poem, "half the house must come down," here, half of his poems must be discarded (either destroyed or repudiated) as, generally speaking, they were. Cavafy's aim, in short, is to root out Romantic excess. Given the Nietzschean relativism of the note on "Truth and Falsehood" of the previous year ("Is there such a thing as Truth and Falsehood? Or is [. . .] Falsehood simply the old age of Truth?"); and after the Wildean note from the same year suggesting that "art always lie[s]," and in fact "the more it lies, the more imaginative it becomes," we might be puzzled to find so much emphasis in the "Scrutiny" on truth and "the necessary truthfulness [of] art." Yet Cavafy's concept of truth (like his use of the word "virtue" elsewhere) is of a particular kind. As we are told in the last paragraph of the main body of the document,

> If a thought has really been true for a day, its becoming false the next day does not deprive it of its claim to verity. It may have been only a passing or a short lived truth, but if intelligent and serious it is worthy to be received, both artistically and philosophically.

Truth, it turns out, is relative; or as Gregory Jusdanis puts it, "local and private."[4] A poem is to be judged not by whether it conforms to existing fact, but by its adherence to the original idea, and by the seriousness and intensity of that idea. Cavafy's use of the term may be closer to our notion of "authenticity," a question of being "true" to an insight or an intuition.

Cavafy continued to review his poems throughout our period; according to Diana Haas's estimate, "reports" on twenty-six poems survive from these years.[5] Some of the Notes included here apparently derive from the "Scrutiny" project. One note written only a few days after the postscript to that document concludes, "This proves the verity of 'Satrapy.'" Another presents itself as "proof to the verity of 'An Old Man.'" Still another note clearly issues from the same set of concerns, though it shows an attention to audience not present in the "Scrutiny": "If my poems lack general applicability, they at least possess a partial one. That is no small thing. Their verity is thereby guaranteed." Such remarks make it clear that, in addition to his concern with both empirical and performative "truths," Cavafy was at the same time endeavoring to articulate a minority poetics.

Nietzsche and the quickening pulse of the new century (abetted perhaps by the small jolt of turning forty) empowered Cavafy to undertake this review and radical purge of his work (his austere 154-poem "canon" is one result of this process). An equally important catalyst may have been his three-month trip to Athens in the fall of 1903, where most of the "Scrutiny" is thought to have been written. It seems probable that Cavafy's encounters among the intellectual elite of Athens triggered a desire to articulate a theoretical

---

4. Jusdanis, *The Poetics Of Cavafy: Textuality, Eroticism, History* (Princeton, N.J.: Princeton University Press, 1987), 110.

5. Haas, "Cavafy's Commentaries on his Poems," in *Cavafy Cycle* (Athens: Moraitis, 1983), 90.

platform from which to speak about poetry, and his own poetry in particular. But the Athens trip was catalytic in another way too. If century's turn encouraged Cavafy to break free of convention and begin addressing matters of deepest importance to himself, as in the three Notes from late 1902, it was a young Athenian named Alexis Mavroudis who precipitated a similar breakthrough in his poems.

All we know about Cavafy's acquaintance with Mr. Mavroudis—an otherwise forgotten figure of the Athenian (and later Parisian) literary scene—we learn from four texts from the fall and winter of 1903-1904. We first encounter him in the addendum to the "Scrutiny," where Cavafy speaks of "the great crisis of libidinousness succeeding on my departure from Athens."[6] The passage continues, "Now, say that in time Ale. Mav. comes to be indifferent to me,[7] like Sul. (I was very much in love with him before my departure for Athens) or Bra." Here at a stroke we are given, in abbreviated form, the names of three of Cavafy's objects of affection or desire, if not lovers. More telling still are the three unpublished "Month" poems—"September 1903," "December 1903," and "January 1904"—that are the subject of the quoted passage. Given that each of the three poems bears the penciled initials "A. M.," it becomes possible to correlate the origin of Cavafy's homoerotic love poetry to his libidinal "crisis" after leaving Athens, presumably brought on by Alexis Mavroudis.

Among the most directly personal of all of Cavafy's poems, these three "hidden" poems mark an appreciable advance in expressive immediacy. Still, there is nothing in the poems themselves to tip us off as to the gender of the beloved—a trait they share with many another poem in the Petrarchan tradition, not least the sonnets of Shakespeare. If not for the initials, and their association with a name in the "Scrutiny" text, the identity of the "you" addressed in the second and third poem would remain as dark as

---

6. This conjectural reading has been adopted by others as well. What the manuscript has is "cr. of lib.," and this seems the most promising solution—preferable to alternatives like "crapulence of libations" proposed by the text's original editor. G. P. Savidis's "crisis of liberation" is a more promising alternative, though it smacks of a later era.

7. That is, someone of indifference to me.

Shakespeare's mistress. With its poignant refrain—"so close, so many times"—"September 1903" could be a poem about any missed opportunity and subsequent regret. Yet by the opening line of the second poem—"And if I can't speak of my love"—it is clear we are dealing with a "love that dare not speak its name." While not examples of his best work, this trio of poems constitutes a watershed because, despite the claim in "December 1903" of not being able to talk about his love, here for the first time Cavafy does just that. The effect was decisive: the poems, dated to January 1904 (though two were drafted earlier) were followed by as many as seven poems from the same year of a plainly erotic character (two of which survive only as titles). This number rises to eight, if we include the historical poem "Orophernes," with its "voluptuous Ionian nights" where one could "[taste] pleasure to the full extent" among "beautiful Ionian youths."

Cavafy never again indulged in the same degree of emotional candor as he had in the "Month" poems; still, in the affective and cognitive process they enact—from the apprehension of irremediable loss to compensatory acts of memory and imagination—these three poems set the pattern for many of the later erotic poems. It is certainly worth pondering that Cavafy's career as a poet of homosexual desire was inaugurated by a triad of poems about a love affair that appears not to have taken place.

So 1904 did indeed mark the beginning of something new, though this something had its start in the forthright challenges or near-challenges to Victorian convention found in several of the 1902 Notes, on subjects like "sexual arousal" and "sexual deviance." In the months that followed the three poems about "A. M.," Cavafy began a series of explicitly erotic (and implicitly homoerotic) poems of such frank realism and uncluttered immediacy as had rarely if ever been seen in post-classical Western poetry. Once again, the poems treat unconsummated desire, but here the attraction is more strictly physical: a figure passed on the stairs of a brothel, another glimpsed in a theater box, yet another in the door of a coffeehouse. If the theme of the earlier poems was proximity ("to have been so close"), the theme of these poems is, significantly, distance. The first and most striking of the poems, "On the Stairs," describes a chance encounter with a stranger on "the disreputable stairs" of a brothel:

As I came down the disreputable stairs, you
were just coming in the door, and for a moment
I saw your unfamiliar face, and you saw me.

Though strangers to one another, their recognition is instantaneous: "Our bodies sensed each other, and sought each other. / Our blood and our flesh understood." Yet confronted with an "other" who is at the same time a mirroring of the self—someone with the same desires, and the same impulse to conceal them—they recoil from the encounter, feeling mutually compromised. Here, the *so close* of "September 1903" becomes *too close*; and as a consequence, "shaken," the figures on the stairs turn away from each other, presumably never to meet again. The manuscript of this unpublished poem bears, not initials, but the penciled label, "unknown."

As if in response, Cavafy's next two poems—"At the Theater" and "In the Entrance to the Café," written in March and July of 1904—keep the erotic figure at a non-threatening distance. The object of desire, glimpsed in a theater box in one, at the door of a café in the other, becomes an object to be admired. The mutuality of eye contact is avoided, thereby safeguarding the integrity of the admiring/desiring subject. In both cases, the speaker's composure hinges on the aestheticization of the love object: his anonymous gaze fixes on the other's physical beauty and youth, even his[8] fine clothing; aesthetic contemplation is enough. "In the Entrance to the Café," on the other hand, literalizes the aesthetic distance by converting the "exquisite body" into a statue fashioned by "Love himself . . . in the fullness of his experience"—a Pygmalion in reverse. In neither poem is there a desire to approach or possess, only the desire to "imagine" and "visualize": the emotional and libidinal disturbances of the "A. M." poems and "On the Stairs" have been mastered through artful distancing. Hereafter, the aesthetic gaze becomes a permanent part of Cavafy's erotic repertoire.

Stories abound that seem to link Cavafy to the sexually active figures that populate his mature poetry. His only biographer, the English novelist Robert Liddell, mentions a brothel where Cavafy purportedly maintained a room, and

8. Or her; here and elsewhere, gender is undefined in Greek.

he notes his preference for Greek rather than Egyptian lovers. Another author tells us of outings in the company of a "young sailor or actor or mechanic."[9] The universal tendency to confuse a writer's work with his or her life is amply at play in discussions of Cavafy the man. It's not unusual to find him characterized as someone who "found unhappy loves in backstreet bars,"[10] an obvious tribute to later poems like "In his Twenty-Fifth Year." It appears that Cavafy abetted this tendency through verbal hints to admirers, and through talks and published articles in which he had a hand. Somewhere there may be evidence aside from hearsay in support of these claims, but if so it has yet to be made public. The available textual evidence indicates that sexual frustration more than anything set the tone for this, his "breakout" period in terms of poetry. In addition to the six poems already discussed, a Note tentatively dated to 1903 speaks of "the enjoyment of love—as I understand & want it," where the context implies such a love is beyond his reach. Then there is the wretched-sounding note in English, probably from 1904 but in any case making reference to January of that year, suggesting that the poet had not even the memory of a single "satisfactory morning or day to my craving for a f[uck]" to console him. Finally, we have testimony to the poet's "almost pathological" shyness that led him to avoid contact with strangers,[11] which does little to support an image of Cavafy as a sexual adventurer.

There is nothing decisive in any of this, but for want of evidence to the contrary, perhaps the most fitting emblem for Cavafy's erotic life at this period is not the boastful celebration of "I Went" ("I was not bound. I let go / completely"), but the more elegiac "Desires" with which the poet marked the end of 1904:

---

9. Liddell, *Cavafy: A Biography* (New York: Schocken Books, 1976), 67-8; Jane Lagoudis Pinchin, *Alexandria Still: Forster, Durrell, and Cavafy* (Princeton, N.J.: Princeton University Press, 1977), 76.

10. Flyer advertising a performance of the play *Days of Cavafy*, which premiered in London in the late 1980s.

11. J. A. Sareyannis, "What Was Most Precious—His Form," trans. Diana Haas, *Grand Street* 2, no. 3 (1983): 124.

Like lovely corpses untouched
by age, sealed amid weeping
in splendid tombs, with jasmine
at the feet, and roses at the head —
such are desires that have gone
unfulfilled, that have never known
a single night of pleasure,
or one of its light-flooded dawns.

The poem's title alone is telling: not "Unfulfilled Desires" (the poem's actual subject) but simply "Desires," as if the two were interchangeable. Cavafy's thwartedness should come as no surprise: he had told us as much in two notes from 1902 ("Clearing the Ground" and "A Single Letter") where he confesses to being cowardly by nature. He would leave *acting* on desires to others, real or imaginary—historical alter egos like Orophernes, for instance, in the poem of that title written the same year, who took his pleasure "fearlessly, [in] true Hellenic spirit." Yet "Desires" is not an expression of the kind of disheveled grief we saw in "September 1903" and "January 1904." Instead, Cavafy seems to feel a certain tenderness toward these stymied impulses, a recognition that they are a thing apart, entities in themselves, and not just negative versions of that absolute: desires fulfilled. They have their own value and integrity. Unsoiled by the temporal, they retain a purity, even a perfection, that acted desires invariably lose in the course of being realized. Enshrined in the mausoleum of memory and art, these eternally deferred desires offer aesthetic consolation, perhaps a unique form of fulfillment. As Margaret Alexiou writes in a perceptive essay on the "Month" poems, "the perspective [alters] from awareness of the emptiness of life to near-realization of desire." She continues, "Poetry can transform the perception of actuality [so that] what has *not* been realized may prove more significant for poetry than 'what actually happened.'"[12] The circularity of Alexiou's formula is true to Cavafy's Art-for-Art's-sake roots, which he never entirely abandoned; still, it sheds little light on what interests me here: the psychical processes that made Cavafy a very different poet in 1911 than he had been in 1902.

12. Alexiou, "Eroticism and Poetry," *Journal of the Hellenic Diaspora* 10, nos. 1-2 (1983): 51.

In poetic terms alone, 1904 was a remarkable year for Cavafy. He had gone from writing no new poems in 1902, to six new poems in 1903, to twelve new poems in 1904—as many as ten of which were on erotic themes. It is his most prolific year of the decade. What makes this all the more remarkable (again, relative to Cavafy's famously slow pace of composition) is that between writing these poems, and rewriting earlier ones, Cavafy persevered in the "philosophical scrutiny" of his earlier work; a number of his "reports" on his poems survive from that year. He also undertook two projects that were an immediate outcome of this self-review: a broadsheet edition of "Waiting for the Barbarians" (which may indicate the importance Cavafy attached to this poem of 1898); and, shortly afterward, the first privately printed and distributed chapbook of his poems.[13] The latter contained 14 poems (but only one, "Desires," from our period), and was printed in an edition of 100. That in turn was superseded in 1910 by another chapbook, printed in an edition of 200 and containing the original 14 poems, plus seven more—but again, with only one addition from our period ("The Retinue of Dionysus"). Such was Cavafy's guarded approach to making his poems—and above all his erotic poems—public. After the 1910 chapbook, Cavafy adopted a more flexible portfolio system of private distribution, whereby poems could be revised, added or deleted, as he gradually and methodically shaped his poetic canon.

While other factors doubtless fueled the creative surge of 1904—an invigorating trip to Athens, an important appreciation of his work in the Athens press[14]—it seems likely that the breakthrough in sexual candor in the

13. The broadsheet resumed a method of distribution he had adopted in the 1890s. It was the last one he did, and G. P. Savidis believes it may never have circulated, being superseded by the chapbook. Sarah Ekdawi suggests that 1903 marks the year Cavafy made up his mind "not to publish commercially or in book form." "'Missing dates': the 'Μέρες' poems of C. P. Cavafy," *Byzantine and Modern Greek Studies* 35, no. 1 (2011): 84.

14. Grigorios Xenopoulos's article in the magazine *Panathenaia* was the first serious consideration of Cavafy's work on the mainland; a moment of recognition to rival Emerson's letter congratulating Whitman on the first edition of *Leaves of Grass*. Xenopoulos was one of the leading lights of the Athens literary scene at the turn of the century.

"Month" poems also played a crucial role. The indications are that Cavafy was working with renewed confidence in his "exceptional abilities" as a poet, and with a firmer sense of his sexual identity. Yet there is another body of writing from this period, mentioned in my introduction, that forms a troubled and for some people potentially troubling counterpart to this image.

CERTAIN IMPEDIMENTS

In "Hidden Things," the unpublished poem of 1908 that gave its name to an entire body of Cavafy's work (*The Hidden Poems*), Cavafy tells us that if we wish to understand him, we must look in the "most veiled" of his writings. Easily the most veiled of Cavafy's writings today are the still-unpublished "confessional notes." What we know of these notes we owe primarily to the 1948 book *The Life and Work of Constantine Cavafy* by Mihalis Peridis. Peridis was an Alexandrian acquaintance who gained possession of at least some of the notes after the poet's death. With genuine reluctance, he discusses their content in a chapter entitled "His Sensual Life."

Peridis has been fulsomely criticized for his unscholarly presentation of those few notes he saw fit to share, but there may have been method in his slipshod approach. Peridis introduces the notes this way:

> I don't think that it is possible for the notes relating to [Cavafy's] erotic declarations to be published in their entirety, whether deciphered or not. Every person has the right to think and perhaps to do anything he likes when it comes to himself, no matter how questionable those things are. It is another matter to make public whatever he thinks or does.
>
> I do not believe that Cavafy intended his confessions for publication. If before he died he didn't destroy them, it is because nobody knows precisely when they will die, and for him the notes constituted a valuable personal document that he would have occasionally gone through and which he didn't wish to banish.
>
> The contents of the confessions are extremely raw and some of their descriptions of an extreme graphic nature that would be more than public consciousness in our age or, I believe, any age could bear.
>
> A few extracts, however, can be made known.[15]

15. Peridis, *The Life and Work of Constantine Cavafy*. (Athens: Ikaros, 1948), 45.

From an ethical perspective, it may be just as well that the notes have been all but inaccessible in the Cavafy Archive in Athens, awaiting decipherment and almost certain publication in a future authorized edition.[16] For better or worse: there's no telling why Cavafy preserved them among his papers, but it certainly wasn't with the aim of future publication. As Peridis notes, they are written for the most part in Cavafy's personal shorthand, using radical abbreviations that can only have been meant as a form of encryption. (Any edition that finally sees print will necessarily involve a good deal of guess work, and very likely many lacunae.) The truth is, writers of a century ago could hardly have envisioned the determination and resourcefulness of the contemporary archival scholar: the academic version of the computer hacker. However that may be, it does seem that Peridis's much criticized sampling gives a fair picture of the general drift of the notes, though we might assume, given his prologue, that he serves up only the mildest examples.

As Peridis understood them, they were the conscience-stricken confessions of a depraved soul, wrestling with his addiction to the same suspect pleasure portrayed in the poems with increasing frankness through the years. They were, Peridis believed, the raw material of the erotic poems: "The verses which express resistance and refusal to submit to this 'sick pleasure' derived directly from the struggle which the poet carried out against it for years on end, and they reflect no more than a small fraction of it" (44). He offers the poem "Understanding" (written 1915, published 1918) as an example:

UNDERSTANDING

The days of my youth,
days of living for the senses,
how clearly I see their meaning now.

What useless repentances —
useless, unavailing . . .

16. In 2012, the privately owned archive was acquired by the Onassis Foundation.

But I didn't see their meaning then.

In the dissipation of my youth,
the inner promptings of my poetry
were being shaped,
the boundaries of my art laid out.

Which is why my repentance never stuck
and my vows to control myself, to change
lasted two weeks at the most.

Peridis took the poem and the notes as reflecting the inner turmoil of a young gay man grappling with his sexuality in late Victorian society, and it is hard to argue with that. When it came to the details, however, he was probably only half right.

Peridis's few extracts stirred up considerable discussion in the ensuing years. A decade after Peridis's book, Stratis Tsirkas, a mid-century novelist and critic out to rehabilitate the poet from a Marxist perspective,[17] gave Cavafy the benefit of the doubt and proposed that the notes documented not aberrant sexuality but a recurring struggle with alcoholism.[18] It took a critic with a less biographical turn on the one hand, and a less ideological agenda on the other—not to mention a founding figure of modern Greek literary studies—to offer an explanation for the notes that is widely accepted today. For Constantine Dimaras, the confessional notes "speak of incomplete erotic experiences, fabricated out of fantasies, desires, and memories, rather than of erotic experiences of an unorthodox kind. For never does another individual appear in these notes; moreover, the external circumstances at times do not seem to favor another individual's presence."[19] Dimaras's sense of delicacy

17. Cavafy's sexual "depravity," like his poetry, had theretofore been seen as a product of bourgeois decadence.

18. Tsirkas, *Cavafy and His Age,* (Athens: Kedros, 1995), 294–98. Nevertheless, Tsirkas is elsewhere happy to imagine Cavafy culling the confessions for useable poetic material.

19. Dimaras, "Cavafy's Technique of Inspiration," trans. Diana Haas. *Grand Street* 2, no. 3 (1983): 146.

forces us to read between his lines, but there can be no mistaking the nature of this "incomplete erotic experience" that dares not speak its name.

Even today, in our enlightened era, masturbation is a topic that is largely avoided in general conversation. For all the fuss about sex in the media, male solo sex is not something that often surfaces as a topic of public discussion, or as a fictional plot element, or a subject in mainstream cinema. As British novelist Martin Amis writes, "Masturbation was an open secret until you were thirty. Then it was a closed secret. Even modern literature shuts up about it at that point, pretty much."[20] Maybe this shouldn't surprise us. From the contemporary perspective, masturbation is the opposite of sex. It is *non*-sex: what you do when you're not getting any. For the adult male, it can be a badge of weakness, exposing one's inability to "score," certainly not one's "exceptional abilities." Though less stigmatized today than it was a hundred years ago, at the time of Cavafy's confessions, it remains under an ethical cloud, even for progressive intellectuals like Slavoj Zizek[21]—all the more surprising, given the recent reversal of medicine's centuries-old wisdom about its effects on one's health.

Most critics of Cavafy have steered clear of the subject, probably for similar reasons. But then, until relatively recently, many Cavafy scholars tiptoed around the subject of Cavafy's sex life altogether. Some of this may be in reaction to the excesses of Cavafy's two earliest biographer-critics, Peridis and Timos Malanos (author of *The Poet C. P. Cavafy* [1934]), who made their conception of the poet's life, not least his erotic life, central to their interpretation of the poetry. In other instances, it may well have been a matter of homophobia, as one recent commentator suggests.[22] For whatever reason, through the years there has been a chorus of critical voices—beginning with George Seferis's "Cavafy doesn't

20. Amis, *London Fields* (New York: First Vintage International Ed., 1991), 67.

21. Echoing eighteenth- and nineteenth-century discourse that tied masturbation to imbecility, Zizek (following Jacques Lacan) singles it out as an "idiot" enjoyment. "Masturbation, or Sexuality in the Atonal World," http://www.lacan.com/symptom/?page_id=247.

22. See George Syrimis, "The History of Tennis," C. P. Cavafy Forum, Modern Greek Program, Department of Classical Studies, University of Michigan.

exist outside of his poetry"[23]—forswearing if not decrying the mixing of life (by implication, sexual life) and letters.

For the purposes of this book, however, it would be a mistake to ignore the existence of the confessional notes and the very real inner struggle they record, if for chronological reasons alone. There is every reason to be wary of these notes: the fact that only some of them have been made public, and the likelihood that these contain errors of transcription. For all that, it seems absurd to dismiss them on ethical or theoretical grounds, or to ignore parallels such as the one Peridis draws between two notes from September of an unknown year—

> I'VE COME TO A GR[EAT] DEC[ISION]. NOW I SW[EAR]! I'm certain of success. Even if just now I gave in . . . We shall see.
> — Sept. 1, 11:30 p.m.
>
> And yet I succumbed again. And now! now! I SW[EAR] AGAIN!!
> — Sept. 10, 11 p.m.

and the poem "He Swears," from December, 1905:

> Every so often he swears
> that he'll start a better life.
> But when night comes on
> with its own advice,
> with its many promises
> and its compromises,
> but when night comes on
> with all the force of
> a body that wants and
> demands — once again
> he abandons himself to the old fatal joy.[24]

---

23. Seferis, "C. P. Cavafy – T. S. Eliot: Parallels," Essays, 3rd ed. (Athens: Ikaros, 1974), 1:362.

24. The connection is reinforced by the Greek word Cavafy uses for "swear" in both cases: the rare *omnýo* rather than the more idiomatic *orkízomé*.

Here one could also introduce the testimony of an outside source, the near contemporary comments of Wilhelm Stekel, a follower of Freud, writing on the negative effects of society's campaign against masturbation:

> Onanists bind themselves by a thousand oaths, by prayers and promises. They have decided not to relapse. This time is the last—and despite the oaths and the promises, they always come back to their instinct.[25]

Alexiou, in the article mentioned previously, finds Peridis's methods "sordid, morbid and horrid," though it is not clear whether she was aware of the confessional notes' true subject.[26] Given the aims of this book, however—to suggest patterns of Cavafy's writerly development over the course of a crucial decade—it would be wrong not to take into account the persistence of the notes, however elusive they are materially, and the personal struggle they expose, however inconvenient conceptually. If I spend more time on this than the casual reader or admirer of Cavafy might like, it is partly because, however much the subject has been alluded to, it has never really been seriously analyzed. Yet the intensity of the confessional notes suggests that this knot at the center of his life occupied Cavafy emotionally, and by extension imaginatively, during this ten-year period. Likewise, as I will show, its ultimate unraveling had much to do with his self-acceptance as an artist. By the end of the decade he had developed a conceptual frame that could contain these dissonant elements of self, just as earlier he had made a place for his gay selfhood with the help of the insurgent discourses of turn-of-the-century Europe. After 1911, when the confessional notes cease, it truly does become irrelevant to the poetry.

Masturbation is a temptation in the best of times, and how much more so

---

25. Quoted in Jean Stengers and Anne Van Neck, *Masturbation: History of a Great Terror*, trans. Kathryn Hoffmann (New York: Palgrave, 2001), 118.

26. Alexiou, "Eroticism and Poetry," 46. Alexiou is repelled by Peridis's literal-minded "correlation between the poem 'He Swears' [. . .] and Cavafy's private and cryptic noctural jottings [. . .]—never meant for the eyes of prurient critics." (Alexiou mistakenly directs her outrage at Stratis Tsirkas, whom she attacks elsewhere in the same article.)

for someone in Cavafy's position: a homosexual living on the fringes of high bourgeois society, with the recent example of Oscar Wilde's trial to remind him how quickly social tolerance could dissolve into condemnation and ostracism. In the words of fellow Alexandrian J. A. Sareyannis,

> Before 1914, in his city and particularly within his class, there prevailed an imitation of Victorian morality [...]. In such an atmosphere, a scandal such as that of Oscar Wilde could easily have been repeated. Cavafy ran the risk of seeing his relatives' homes closed to him, of being ostracized, of no longer being greeted on the street, or even ... being banished from the city he loved. (125)

It might well have been different if he had lived in a major European center like Paris, where he conceivably could have discovered a community of kindred souls. There is no record of his ever having belonged to such a circle of shared identity in Alexandria. Of his hometown Cavafy wrote, "[H]ow it oppresses me. What a hardship, what a burden a small city is. What a curb on one's freedom. [...] [H]ow much someone like me—different as I am—needs a big city."[27] When to these circumstantial elements we add Cavafy's self-avowed timidity, it seems natural that he should fall back on this less risky channel of sexual release, if not fulfillment. Here we come close to critic John Anton's no-nonsense formulation of the case, which brackets masturbation and alcohol as escape valves for sexual pressure: "It would hardly be an exaggeration to say that his [Cavafy's] eroticism is the most misunderstood and most discussed aspect of his personality. He never was much of a 'brave man of pleasure' [...]. The fact is that in real life he dissipated the fervor of the drive through the use of alcohol and self-indulgence."[28] Yet, as the anguish of the notes suggests, Cavafy's "self-indulgence" was more than just a physiological phenomenon. If Cavafy had at least conceptually accepted himself as a homosexual at the

27. Note from April 28, 1907.

28. John P. Anton, *Poetry and Poetics of Constantine P. Cavafy: Aesthetic Visions of Sensual Reality* (Chur, Switz.: Harwood, 1995), 267.

beginning of our period, he had a harder time with this other facet of his sexuality. It was a secret that weighed heavily on him, one that sent ripples through all aspects of his life and, as I will show, exerted a shaping pressure on his poetry.

To understand the surprising weight of this secret, it helps to have a sense of the anti-onanist discourse as it existed in the West at the turn of the last century. Masturbation had been a target of moral and pseudo-scientific screeds for centuries, yet as Lesley A. Hall writes in the *Journal of the History of Sexuality*, "The era of greatest masturbation anxiety was not (as is usually thought) the mid-Victorian period but the late Victorian to Edwardian era, indeed up to the outbreak of World War I"[29]; in other words, precisely the period of Cavafy's desperate late-night scribbles. Cavafy lived in what Hall describes as "a climate of opinion that blamed masturbation for a variety of ailments from warts on the fingers to impotence, consumption, convulsions, insanity, and death" (376)—or, indeed, "ills more terrible than even death," as one nineteenth-century savant assures us.[30] Even an early debunker of such myths, the noted Victorian surgeon James Paget, expresses regret at having to do so; for him, the practice remained "an uncleanliness, a filthiness forbidden by God, an unmanliness despised by men."[31]

Given the tenor of those times, one can almost understand Dimaras's point when, in the article cited above, he goes on to suggest that the homosexuality of Cavafy's poems and personal mystique was a cover for an even greater shame.

---

29. Hall, "Forbidden by God, Despised by Men: Masturbation, Medical Warnings, Moral Panic, and Manhood in Great Britain, 1850–1950." *Journal of the History of Sexuality* 2, no. 3 (1992): 371.

30. Fournier and Béguin as quoted in Vernon A. Rosario II, M. D., "Phantastical Pollutions: The Public Threat of Private Vice in France," in *Solitary Pleasures: The Historical, Literary, and Artistic Discourses of Autoeroticism*, ed. Paula Bennett and Vernon A. Rosario II (New York, London: Routledge, 1995), 110.

31. Sir James Paget, "Sexual Hypochondriasis," *Clinical Lectures and Essays*, ed. Howard Marsh (New York: D. Appleton and Co., 1875), 285.

> [B]y coming forth with one morally condemned passion, [Cavafy] is able to bring to completion his lyrical confession and at the same time to conceal another passion, also condemned. The first one does not offend human pride, while the second is degrading; the first has been celebrated by many from antiquity to the present, while the second one by very few.[32]

There is an element of truth here, but to imply, as this passage does, that homosexuality plays a secondary, diversionary role in the poems is to misunderstand or misrepresent the nature of sexuality in general, and of Cavafy's sexuality in particular. Whether or not Cavafy practiced autoeroticism in his spare time makes him neither more nor less of a homosexual, though people might disagree over the number of his actual sexual encounters. In the end, these two aspects—his homosexuality and his "autosexuality"—are one. Because of who he was, sexually and otherwise, and the world he inhabited, Cavafy found himself unable to have the active and meaningful sex life he would have liked. His temperament made him unwilling to risk social scandal, or to submit to the demeaning conditions under which active homosexuals were forced to operate. "Certain impediments stood in the way," he writes in "Hidden Things," "transforming my actions and my manner of life." This poem is usually discussed as a comment on Cavafy's poetic practice, and on his suppression of some of his most explicit poems (most of them included here). But as this passage suggests, it applies at least as much to the speaker's personal life. The intricacies of anyone's imaginative or actual sex life are infinite, and this is certainly true for Cavafy. So it's a pity that recent investigations into the homoerotic element in the poetry have either shunned its autoerotic counterpart altogether or, in one case, dismissed it as a homophobic red herring. I would argue that it is impossible to consider the one without considering the other: Cavafy's homoerotic content was matched with an autoerotic aesthetic. In other words, his manner of coming to terms with the latter on a personal level helped shape his *creative* treatment of the other in

32. Dimaras, "Inspiration," 146.

the more public sphere of poetry. In the next section, I trace the nuances of this dynamic of two elements that were both the same and different, different but the same.

* * *

The veiled nature of the eroticism in Cavafy's poems, especially in the earliest of his *printed* erotic poems, has been much commented on. Because of the need for self-censorship, Cavafy cultivated a degree of indirectness, of abstraction, even of vagueness in his verse that left the nature of his eroticism undisclosed. Poems like "I Swear" and "Understanding" give nothing away; they could apply to almost any form of overindulgence, from an intemperate craving for chocolate to the most extreme Sadean excess. The same applies to "Dangerous Pursuits" (1911), identified as the first "daring" poem Cavafy ever published. The poem's Greek title (*Ta Epikíndhina*) consists of a substantive adjective (neuter plural) meaning literally "dangerous [things]." As in the similarly titled "Hidden [Things]" (*Krymmena*) of 1908, the referent is omitted; it is left to the reader to decide *what* is hidden, *what* is dangerous. Stripped of the historical frame in its opening four lines, "Dangerous Pursuits" is—if not a confession—then an avowal of sorts, but now in the forthright terms of the poem "Growing Strong in Spirit" ("He will have much to learn from pleasure") and some of the earlier Notes ("I feel that I possess exceptional abilities"):

> Fortified by study and contemplation,
> I will not go in cowardly fear of my passions,
> I will give my body entirely to pleasure,
> to all the things that I've dreamed about,
> to the wildest promptings of my flesh,
> the secret urges of my blood — without
> the least fear, because I know that
> when I set my mind to it — and I *will*,
> fortified as I'll be by study and contemplation —
> at crucial moments my ascetic spirit
> will come back to me, undiminished.

Again, what those dreamed-of delights might be we can only guess. In a 1918 lecture probably traceable to Cavafy himself, his protégé Alekos Sengopoulos remarks of the poem: "The truth is [the poet] could not reveal any more. He spells these matters out only to the degree possible."[33] Whatever carnal acts the speaker of the poem envisions, Cavafy's title hangs a caution sign on them: what is "dangerous," it turns out, is Pleasure. To give in to the promptings of the flesh, to the secret urges of the blood, is to tempt fate. Once released, one's sensual proclivities are not easily kept in harness, as the confessional notes amply attest.

Cavafy didn't invent the turn-of-the-century cult of Pleasure, but he made as effective use of it as anyone. The Greek word for pleasure, *hēdonē*, is the root of our hedonism, but its popularity among fin-de-siècle writers can be traced to Baudelaire's homage to "la volupté" in *Fleurs du Mal.* (Cavafy's first ode to voluptas is a Baudelairean prose poem from 1896 entitled "The Regiment of Pleasure.") The British Aesthetes took it up, most notably Oscar Wilde in *The Picture of Dorian Gray.* ("I have never searched for happiness. Who wants happiness? I have searched for pleasure.") Exactly what form these voluptuous pleasures took is rarely spelled out, though it was understood that whatever they might be, they were not of the "routine" variety enjoyed within the confines of marriage, or in the service of human reproduction.[34] Just as Hellenism became for Pater and Wilde, and later for Cavafy, a vehicle for expressing forbidden desires, so Pleasure in the fin-de-siècle carried with it the scent of forbidden fruit: it might be sibling incest, or a languid lesbianism;

---

33. Sengopoulos, "Lecture on the Poetic Work of C. P. Cavafy." *Review of the Arts [Epitheorisi Tehnis]* 18: 108 (Dec. 1963), 617. Other comments by Sengopoulos/Cavafy about the poem oddly echo the anti-onanist cant of the period: "Such a life [. . .] will consume all of one's youth." True, there may be interruptions, but "they will unquestionably be interruptions caused by fatigue, if not temporary exhaustion. [. . .] Is it possible that leading such a life, going from one pleasure to the next, will not weaken one's character?" Masturbation was seen at the time as dangerously addictive and ultimately enfeebling.

34. "My life's joy and incense: that I shunned / every routine form of pleasure," writes Cavafy in "To Pleasure." Elsewhere he speaks of a "sterile kind of love." Lord Henry Wotton, in Oscar Wilde's *The Picture of Dorian Gray*, refers vaguely to "beautiful sins."

just as often, though, the specifics were left to the imagination. This stylistic elusiveness, inspired in part by censorship concerns, played into Cavafy's hand on two levels. In a Note from December 1905, Cavafy laments that, on account of the "miserable laws of society," he must remain "an object of speculation," divined only in what his poems leave out. Writing a few years later, however, Cavafy finds a silver lining: "Fortunately, [my] poems are often cryptic; thus other—comparable—feelings or states of mind can easily be made to fit them." And early Greek readers of Cavafy's erotic poems were happy to do just that.[35] We find an image of this speculative process, again channeled through ancient history, in the poem "One of their Gods," drafted just before and published just after our period. There, certain residents of Hellenistic Seleucia, noticing a beautiful young stranger passing down their street on his way to "the district that comes alive / only at night, with orgies and excess, / and every form of drunkenness and lust," and surmising that he is one of the gods, wonder "what form of pleasure" he's come down from Olympus in pursuit of; presumably each of the observers comes up with his or her own answer. Knowledge may be power, but knowledge withheld has its own kind of power, and an "object of speculation" is by nature magnetic.

There is a sophisticated algebra at work in these poems, whereby Pleasure A is folded into Pleasure B, which in turn is projected as a vaguely defined Pleasure C. (Cavafy's first openly *homo*erotic poem was published in 1922.) In celebrating one proscribed pleasure, the poet makes space for another, *personally* abhorred pleasure, under a capacious banner that provides coverage for both. The emergent European discourse of transgressive sexuality in the early years of the century allowed Cavafy to re-imagine a source of sexual shame as an act of supreme social nonconformity, as the sphere of homoerotic desire merged with the world of autoerotic practice.

Given this fluidity of terms, it should come as no surprise that the imagination is given such a prominent place in Cavafy's erotic poetry: it is the

35. I have been assured that, until relatively recently (I would imagine since the days of gay liberation), it was possible to read Cavafy's poems in Greek without suspecting their sexual orientation.

great facilitator. The presiding deity of the Aesthetics and Decadents, who took to heart Walter Pater's injunction to honor "imaginative enjoyment" above all else, Imagination was also the ultimate villain of much anti-onanistic literature (along with tight clothing, bicycle seats, and romantic novels). "[W]hat made masturbation so threatening," writes Thomas Laqueur, was that it "entailed the willful mobilization of the imagination to engage in the endless creation of desire."[36] Laqueur marshals two centuries' worth of authorities (including Kant and Freud) who finger the imaginative faculty as "the artisan [of] the fatal rage of Masturbation."[37] The phantasmal images on which the act was understood to depend threatened to supplant the legitimate object of desire. Reproductive imperatives aside, the autonomous libidinal economy this implied threatened the integrity of the social mechanism; for Freud, civilization began with the suppression of the masturbatory impulse.

Increasingly, Cavafy took a contrarian stance, making more and more room for the imagination in his formulation of the erotic. He had affirmed its supremacy in strictly aesthetic terms as early as 1886, in the poem "Poet and Muse," but his first profession in an erotic context came in the 1905 poem "I Went," where the speaker tells us he gave himself to pleasures that were "half real, half spun in my brain." Here again we are left no wiser as to the nature of these half-imagined pleasures, since the poem ends with one of Cavafy's very few flights into metaphor: "And I drank of heady wine, / such as the lords of pleasure drink." Not until a decade later was Cavafy able to capture in verse one such instance of half-and-half pleasure, in an unpublished poem from 1916 titled, appropriately, "Half an Hour."

---

36. Laqueur, *Solitary Sex: A Cultural History of Masturbation* (New York: Zone Books, 2004), 220.

37. D. T. de Bienville, *Dictionnaire portatif de santé*, 2: 340, quoted in Laqueur, *Solitary Sex*, 215. For Kant, the problem with the masturbatory imagination was that it "brings forth an appetite contrary to nature's purpose" (214). Freud's worry was that it "contributes to the substitution of fantasy objects for real objects" (210). "On the Universal Tendency to Debasement in Love." *The Standard Edition of the Complete Psychological Works of Sigmund Freud*, trans. James Strachey (London: Hogarth, 1953-74), 11: 182.

HALF AN HOUR

I never had you — nor, I'm afraid,
will I ever have you. A few words, a brush
of the shoulder — as at the bar the other night —
and that is all. A pity, I admit.
And yet sometimes, we who serve art,
through sheer intensity of thought,
and of course only for a little while,
are able to create a pleasure
that seems almost material.

As at the bar the other night — helped,
to be sure, by the mercies of alcohol —
I experienced half an hour that was
supremely erotic. And I think
you understood this, and stayed
a little longer on my account.
This too was necessary. Because
for all the powers of the imagination,
and for all the sorcery of drink,
I needed to see your lips as well,
I needed to feel your body's nearness.

Here the poet-speaker, through "the powers of the imagination," is "able to create a pleasure / that seems almost material." And yet the imagination couldn't do it alone; the physical fact of the other's presence—along with an infusion of alcohol—is a necessary supplement. In 1904, Cavafy might have classified this experience as yet another "unfulfilled" desire (he didn't "have" the person in question), and consigned it to the sad mausoleum along with all the rest. But by 1916 he had begun to credit such liminal forms of eroticism, and imagination's legitimate role in bringing out their full potential. In poems like "Half an Hour" and "Remember, Body" from the previous year—where the body is instructed to remember "not just the beds you shared" but also the desires that were thwarted by some "chance obstacle"—Cavafy is evolving a new erotics of the mind, where the potential of a sexual or sexually-charged encounter is realized only through the artist's imaginative interventions.[38] Ultimately it is not the act itself—what did or did not occur—that matters, but the inner experience—whatever the source—and what the poetic imagination is able to make of it. Three poems from the end of our period crystallize an important phase in this evolving aesthetics.

SECRECY, EXCESS, AND IMAGINATION

Laqueur suggests a discursive link between onanism and homosexuality on the grounds that, historically, both "seemed to lie in the shadows of secrecy, excess, and the imagination" (267). However slender this connection in real terms, the three qualities Laqueur cites—secrecy, excess, and the imagination—seem chosen with Cavafy's particular form of eroticism in mind. As it happens, these three terms can be applied individually to each of the three poems I turn to now, all dating from the final year of our period. In the first of these, "Hearing of Love," written in June 1911 but never published, Imagination is given the place of honor. As with the earlier "In the Entrance to the Café" ("Something I heard") and "At the Theater" ("things I'd heard"), "Hearing of Love" is triggered by something heard:

---

38. The proportions were not always so evenly split, as an unfinished poem from 1922 makes clear:

> . . . Imagination, taking
> something — the littlest bit — from life:
> a distant vignette, a long-ago moment
> of pleasure, brought a vision of its own,
> a vision of the flesh, to the amorous bed.
> ("Birth of a Poem")

Here, "real-life" experience serves as no more than the grit in the oyster. As the title tells us, the outcome of this erotic transaction between memory and the imagination is not a child but a poem. See *Unfinished Poems: 1918-1932*, edited by Renata Lavagnini (Athens: Ikaros, 1993), 123.

HEARING OF LOVE

When you hear of passionate love, tremble
and be moved, like an esthète.
But afterwards remember, with contentment,
all the things imagination shaped for you: these
remember first; and then the rest, the lesser things,
tangible and more real, that life has given you
to experience and enjoy.
You had your share of such loves too.

The poem "Remember, Body," mentioned earlier, identifies two forms of erotic experience—consummated and not—and while it was primarily interested in the second of these—impeded desire—it chose no favorites between the two. Not so "Hearing of Love." Here, those experiences which "the imagination shaped for you" are contrasted with the other kind, "tangible and more real," that have been lived in flesh and in fact. The latter—the "real" experiences—are cast as secondary and inferior: somehow "lesser" or "smaller" pleasures that come as little more than an afterthought ("and then the rest") to the poem's reflexive boast about nonphysical, imagined sex; sex, that is, not requiring "another individual's presence." We may wonder at the psychology of this—why the speaker should have such a response to someone else's passionate love affair—but of greater interest here is the way the poem dares to invert the conventional hierarchies of love, passion, and sex, by privileging fantasy over the "real" thing: "*these* / remember first; and then the rest." It would be easy enough to take such passages as the residual gestures of an erstwhile Aesthete—enamored, like Pater, of "things of the intellect and the imagination for their own sake"[39]; after all, as recently as 1903 Cavafy had been reworking one last time—before consigning it to his drawer—an 1895 poem extolling "Artificial Flowers" over real ones. But what happens if, instead of reflecting the artistic fashions of the prior century, we understand Cavafy's

39. Walter Pater, *The Renaissance: Studies in Art and Poetry,* ed. Donald L. Hill (Berkeley, Calif.: University of California Press, 1980), xxiv-xxv.

stance as foreshadowing the theoretical concerns of our own era? It is possible to see Cavafy not simply as an ec-centric modernist emerging from the creative ferment of the fin-de-siècle, but as a proto-postmodernist in his preference for wry micronarratives and, as here, his careful undermining of hierarchical oppositions like "real" and "imagined." In the end, in a poem like "Hearing of Love," the imagined outmaneuvers the real, the supplemental becomes primary.[40] If we then reinsert the poem back into its historical context — I'm thinking especially of the anti-masturbation cant of the day — we can grasp how calculated and subversive Cavafy's embrace of the erotic imagination was.

Furthering his counterintuitive challenge to what constitutes "legitimate" experience, Cavafy wrote a poem four months later that more than any other confounds the two — real and imaginary sex — and that works to undermine the very distinction between them. Again, I give the poem in full, since I want to go through it in some detail.

I HAVE GAZED SO LONG —

I have gazed so long at beauty
that it has come to fill all my vision.

Lines of the body. Red lips. Amorous limbs.
Hair as if copied from Greek statues —
lovely to look at, always, even uncombed
and falling, just slightly, over the white
forehead. Shapes of love, as my poetry
wanted them ... in the nights of my youth,
encountered, secretly, in my nights ...

If "Hearing of Love" took us back to two poems, "In the Entrance to the Café" and "At the Theater," likewise triggered by something (over)heard, this poem recalls the same two poems by its emphasis on the gaze. The

40. See Jacques Derrida's chapter in *Of Grammatology* on Rousseau's "dangerous supplement." (Part II, chapter 2).

opening two-line stanza in particular repays attention, a baroque confection of archaizing morphology, inversions and vocabulary that might baffle even native speakers not accustomed to Cavafy's stylistic oddities. A literal rendering of the lines gives us:

> [Upon] beauty so long I've gazed
> That entirely [or crowded] is of it my sight.

Once untangled, the sentence could easily be taken as a simple statement of cause and effect verging on tautology: I look, therefore I see. What is *seen,* however, is unclear since, unlike "At the Theater" and "In the Entrance to the Café," the "scene" of the gaze is left out. "Beauty" appears in the abstract; we have no way of knowing whether it is personified in a living body, as in those two poems; in a work of art (as in "A Crafter of Winebowls"); an obscene photograph (as in "Thus"), or an etching ("In an Old Book"). "I Have Gazed So Long —" is more a meditation on the gaze itself, as a conduit between the inner and outer worlds, than on any particular act of gazing. The Greek verb *aténisa* ("I gazed") suggests a certain distance from the object, as well as fixity; perhaps only an aesthetic distance, but also possibly a physical one. The word for "vision"—órasis—denotes the physical sense of sight, but there is more than a hint that some crossover or short-circuit has occurred: a confusion of inner and outer, of subjective with objective, where perception and projection are hard to tell apart, as in the better known "Morning Sea": "Let me stop here awhile, and make believe that I really do see these things, / And not, here too, my fantasies, my memories, the conjurings of Eros." Cavafy's realism had its limits.

The opening of the second stanza extends this ambiguity. The bodily attributes offered as examples—lips, limbs, hair—most likely correspond to the objective, gazed-upon "beauty" of the poem's first line, though there is no guarantee that they do not instead refer to their internalized counterparts that "crowd" the speaker's sight in the second line. (The element of artfulness in the descriptions—"lines of the body," the hair likened to that of Greek statues—suggests some form of imaginative mediation.) The ambiguity deepens in the next sentence: "Shapes of love, as my poetry / wanted them." Again, it is possible to take this statement in two ways: either to mean that the speaker's poetry sought out these *particular* "visions" of the beautiful, as its inspiration or raw material; or that his poetry itself (or imagination as its active element) reshaped the features of these (presumably) young men to suit its aesthetic ends.

The final line and a half of the poem carries forward this balancing act, if that is the accurate term when two elements held in balance start to converge: "[I]n the nights of my youth, / encountered, secretly, in my nights . . ." At first, the two references to "nights" appear to be in apposition (as most translators have made them), an instance of Cavafy's penchant for artful repetition, absorbed in all likelihood from his reading of Walt Whitman. Yet in this case, the slight variation in phrasing unsettles any easy equivalence. There is an element of distance to "nights of my youth"—they were *then*, they belong to my youth—while "in my nights" brings them into the present. The phrase "encountered, secretly" applies with certainty to the latter phrase (which it follows in the Greek), and potentially though not necessarily to both; but even if it does apply to both phrases, these two encounters need not be of the same nature: the perhaps *furtive* nocturnal encounters of the poet's youth may have become the *secret* nocturnal encounters of the poet's middle age (Cavafy was nearing fifty when he wrote the poem). The first might suggest physical encounters, either along the lines of "One Night" ("I had love's body") or "Half an Hour" ("I never had you [. . .] And yet"), while the second iteration hints at something more figurative, such as that trumpeted in "Hearing of Love." I would argue that Cavafy's mission in "I Have Gazed So Long —" is to so interfuse the two—real and imaginary Eros—that through the swiftness of the interchange they become one. He achieves a similar sleight-of-hand in a note of 1907, in which he complains that Baudelaire's eroticism "was confined to a very limited circle of pleasure." There Cavafy contrasts his own presumably broader range of pleasure in an especially dense and (in Greek) challenging passage:

> Take last night; or Wednesday past; and how many other times that I have experienced, and carried out, and imagined, and silently orchestrated more unusual forms of gratification.

Like the enumeration of physical features in the second stanza of "I Have Gazed So Long —," the poet's "unusual forms of gratification" are shuffled together in such a way as to make it difficult to recompose them into any coherent sequence or whole. Again, this lack of cohesive order is no more the product of accident or inattention here than in the poem. Both are attempts to render nil the conventional demarcation between the empirical world and the world of the imagination—and in the process between imaginary and material sex. In both instances, Cavafy achieves something close to absolute undecidability. It becomes futile for the reader to try to maintain a clear distinction between a "real and tangible" Eros, and a solitary Eros activated by the imaginative powers. Cavafy has broken down the wall between the two by means of an ambiguity at once syntactic and semantic. "I Have Gazed So Long —" is not one of Cavafy's "split" poems (see "To Antiochus Epiphanes" here, and "The City" and "A Prince from Western Libya" in his collected poems), yet there seems to be a scarcely perceptible seam or fold running through its length, occluding any sure point of orientation and deferring any final reading.[41]

By giving Imagination, bugbear of the anti-masturbationists, pre-eminence in his formulation of the erotic, Cavafy truly did free himself from his own "bonds of superstition," while also striking a blow against convention in the name of a nonconformist aestheticism. The Greek critic Dimaras, as we saw,

---

41. Of the many English translators of this poem, there are two who seem to be responding to this semantic stammer. First, John Mavrogordato, one of Cavafy's earliest translators, gives us this odd rendering of the opening two lines: "So much I gazed on beauty gazing / My vision is full of it full of beauty." Fifty years later, Theoharis C. Theoharis sprinkles doublets throughout: "I've gazed *so long, so much*"; "*Faces* and *persons* of love"; and, in the final line, "in those nights of mine, *furtive, secretly* encoutered" (emphasis mine). Here, an apparent indecisiveness on the translator's part may in fact reflect the discursive slippage of the original. Mavrogordato, *The Poems of C. P. Cavafy* (New York: Random House, 1951), 88; Theoharis, trans., *Before Time Could Change Them: The Complete Poems of Constantine P. Cavafy* (New York: Harcourt, 2001), 68.

hinted that Cavafy deployed homosexuality as a screen to conceal an even more shame-ridden vice, yet these poems suggest the contrary: that Cavafy was eager to foreground the importance of imaginary sex, to affirm its experiential validity and claim a place for it in the lexicon of literary eroticism.

What does this mean in terms of my narrative of "clearing the ground" and the more general tradition (initiated by the poet himself) of identifying 1911 as the year of Cavafy's "arrival"? By merging these two forms of shunned sexuality—one involving perceived overindulgence, the other avowed deprivation—and subsuming them both under the sign of Pleasure, Cavafy found a way to reconceive a sexual practice that for over ten years had caused him untold psychological and psychosomatic anguish, as the confessional notes suggest, and as the records show it had for many a man and woman over the course of two centuries and more. By destabilizing the binary terms of real and imagined, as he does in "I Have Gazed So Long —," *and* increasingly asserting the legitimacy of liminal or parasexual experiences, as in "Half an Hour," "Remember, Body," and "Hearing of Love," Cavafy, it seems, came to accept the dual realities of his sexual existence "without"—to borrow from a later poem—"any ridiculous feelings of shame over what form his pleasure took."[42] His last two confessional notes date from the fall of 1911.

In 1898 Cavafy had published a poem, "An Old Man," in which the elderly subject sits alone with his ruined body in a café and, in a Chekhovian moment, reflects on

> how little he enjoyed the years
> when he had strength, and wit, and looks.
>
> ◆ ◆ ◆
>
> He thinks back to urges he stifled, joys
> he sacrificed. Each missed opportunity
> now mocks his foolish prudence.

---

42. "He Came to Read" (1924), described by Mark Lilly as a "masturbation poem." Lilly, *Gay Men's Literature in the Twentieth Century* (New York: New York University Press, 1993), 45.

In a Note from 1906, Cavafy wrote:

> You sit down and write — often by guess work — about experiences, then as time goes by you begin to wonder whether you weren't misled. I wrote "Candles," "The Souls of Old Men," and "An Old Man" about old age. Approaching old age — or middle age — I've realized that the last of these poems does not give an accurate account of it.

Five years later, in December of 1911, Cavafy wrote the poem that ends this collection, and that can be seen as a possible alternative or corrective to the earlier poem's "[in]accurate account." Once again the subject is an elderly and evidently solitary man, in this case returning home—conceivably from the very same café as in "An Old Man." He too feels the indignity of being old. This time, however, instead of regrets about his unlived youth, we get "A Rare Exception":

> Spent, bent down,
> ravaged by the years and bad living,
> he slowly makes his way across the street.
> But as he turns in at his door, as he shuts
> his decrepitude and age from view, he considers
> the stake he still has in youth.

What the old man dwells on here is not the youth that has passed him by, but rather the youth (plural) who are reciting his verses in the present. Approaching middle age, Cavafy is able to visualize a different future for himself—for there is little doubt that he is projecting his own future here. Still alone, true, still physically a shambles as in the earlier poem, but now partially compensated by the thought that his verse might really outlast him. While the first stanza details his body's wretchedness—his bent, crippled form—the tone of the second stanza is triumphant:

Now it's *his* verses the young recite,
his visions that fill their vivid eyes.
Their healthy and sensuous minds
and sturdy, well-molded flesh
are moved by his own articulation of the beautiful.

There is something decidedly Platonic in this image of Age bequeathing its visions to the "healthy and sensuous minds" of the young—a mixture of the paternal and the erotic. Perhaps the young, in their turn, will be able to convert his words—"the words of a coward"—into actions, as in the 1902 Note I looked at earlier. This is one consolation. The other consolation resides in the word "catachresis," which I translate in the second line as "bad living."

Ancient rhetoricians and modern critics employ "catachresis" to mean the misuse of a word, whether from ignorance or by design. In modern Greek, however, it is used more widely to mean "abuse," as in the phrases "drug abuse" or "abuse of privileges." In the poem it obviously means abusing the body through excess, through doing things one shouldn't—things Prudence and the health manuals warned us against, or the sapient laws of society forbid. I hope it's clear by now that whatever active gay sex life Cavafy might have enjoyed, it was unlikely to have been as excessive as "catachresis" implies here. If Cavafy knew excess, it was more likely to have been in the direction of alcohol and masturbation, the latter dubbed "self-abuse" in the sexual purity tracts of the time. I don't want to insist too much on this reading, any more than the poem itself does; for ultimately it belongs to biography, and with the poetry the distinction hardly matters. But in terms of the creative narrative I have drawn from this gathering of ten years' worth of writing, I would like to see closure in the fact that in November 1911, Cavafy wrote the last known confessional note, and a month later wrote a poem in which unnamed forms of (self) abuse are seen to be redeemed by one's poetic achievement.

After that, the private Cavafy largely disappears into the figure of the poet.

◆ ◆ ◆

Passions and Ancient Days was the well-chosen title of the first English selection of Cavafy's posthumous poems (known in Greece as *The Hidden Poems*) and it nicely covers the range of poetic themes in the present selection. Yet in my attempt to sketch a dialogue between his prose and his poetry, my focus has been almost exclusively on the "Passions." I have scarcely touched on the second component—"Ancient Days"—in this essay, even though until relatively recently this had been Cavafy's major claim to fame. (For whatever reason, there is only one passing mention of antiquity in the Notes.)[43] At the same time, as has often been pointed out, keeping the two categories separate is difficult, given that sensuality and homoeroticism are so much a part of Cavafy's ancient world.

Cavafy had many reasons for availing himself of historical material from late antiquity—not least his being a Greek from Alexandria—but surely being gay played a large part in it. As it had for the Oxford Hellenists before him, the ancient world afforded a venerable stage on which male beauty and same-sex love could be represented and even celebrated in a determinedly heterosexual world. Earlier, I voiced doubt about Dimaras's contention that the homosexuality of the poetry was meant to disguise the real subject, the autoeroticism of the life, but it's clear that Hellenism did provide a sort of camouflage for the homoerotic content of the poems. But even that's not quite right. Using the medium of the Hellenistic world, Cavafy was able to advance his project of achieving ever greater freedom of expression, despite the "miserable laws of society" in his day. Edmund Keeley has written insightfully about the "pattern of revelation" that Cavafy adopted for the distribution and publication of his poems, in which he administered Mithridatic doses of the homoerotic to gradually inoculate his readers against potential moral shock.[44]

43. "I go about it like the ancients. They wrote history, philosophy, mythological dramas of the tragic, driven — so many of them — by desire . . . just like me." Note from June 20, 1910.

44. The dissemination of his poems, Keeley continues, "was carefully controlled so that it progressed in stages from the general and implicit to the more specific and overt." Keeley, *Cavafy's Alexandria* (Princeton, N. J.: Princeton University Press, 1996), 45.

(This may explain the obtrusion of homoerotic elements in poems like "Alexandrian Kings" and "Aristovolos," where they are not strictly demanded by the material.) His purpose in doing so, as Keeley points out, was "more than merely personal"; but neither was it ultimately in the service of a "mythical method," as Keeley argues.[45] Rather, it was the reverse. As the Notes make clear, the impulse behind the combined strategies of camouflage and graduated divulgence was to provide encouragement "to others who are made like me"; and ultimately "to make it easier for [them] to act." His purpose, in other words, was to "clear the ground," so that in the future, "someone made like me" could "come forward and act freely." True, this reliance on the historical might give the impression that the "more perfect society" envisioned by the ameliorism of "Hidden Things" was in fact situated in the remote past, in the sexually more tolerant Greek world of the Hellenistic Age—an age in which, Cavafy is quoted as saying, his imagination felt at home.[46] The result is a reversal of the gentle dialecticism of the 1902 Note that supplied the title for this book and that has served as a touchstone for this essay. There, Cavafy had expressed his faith that the words of the present might "clear the ground" for the actions of the future. In this other version, past actions, past realities—the world of antiquity—make possible the words of the present. Had Cavafy, by 1911, become a nostalgist, a cultural classicist who believed society's best days were behind it; one who had lost not only the revolutionary fervor of "Growing Strong in Spirit" but also the gradualist spirit of the 1902 Note? Stratis Tsirkas, again writing from a Marxist perspective, says something to this effect:

---

45. "[T]he significant impulse behind his poetic use of anomalous eroticism," Keeley tells us, was a "unique version of the 'mythical method'" that T. S. Eliot originally applied to Joyce's *Ulysses*. Keeley, *Cavafy's Alexandria*, 46.

46. Timos Malanos, *The Poet C. P. Cavafy* (Athens: Drifos, 1957), 77.

> Cavafy's discovery of the "Greek world" after 1910 wasn't a coincidence; it was inevitable. [...] Transporting his subject-identity to that other world, he escaped the monotony and pedestrianism of his life, and consoled himself with the delusion of power for a happiness that had been eaten away in the backstreets of Alexandria. What preoccupies him is no longer action, the great work, but [...] the epitaphic epigram.[47]

Tsirkas offers a partial retraction in his next book, *The Political Cavafy*. But from the point of view of Cavafy's gay activism as well, the historical poems are more than tokens of an "ideology of accommodation and a flight from reality."[48] The ancient world they portray is best understood not as an illusory "other world" substituting for the more perfect society of the future, but as a sort of blueprint that might help that society come into being. Like many a utopian before him, Cavafy in the first decade of the twentieth century looked forward by looking back. Only, to borrow the closing words of a novel much influenced by Cavafy's example, he knew that—for him at least—the time was "not yet ... not there."[49]

47. Tsirkas, *Cavafy and His Age*, 444. Tsirkas is going by dates of publication rather than of composition.

48. Ibid.

49. E. M. Forster, *A Passage to India*. In *Alexandria Still*, Pinchin writes persuasively of Forster's debt in that book to Cavafy, whom he had met in Alexandria during the First World War. See *Alexandria Still*, 223.

IV. APPENDIX
AN UNFINISHED ESSAY **(1906)**

[On The Chronicle of the Morea*]*

One highly gratifying phenomenon of the past few years has been the increased interest among Greeks in their medieval history and literature — in the long and storied Byzantine life of our race. This is not to say that we will now neglect ancient Hellenism. One love does not preclude the other. But it is also right that we should be no less interested — some more so than others — to learn about our fathers, than about our much more prominent grandfathers.

From the many noteworthy books about the medieval phase of our national life that have appeared of late, of especial interest is the new edition by Professor Schmitt, of the University of Leipzig, of the *Chronicle of the Morea,* which Methuen, the major London publishing firm, beautifully and meticulously produced the year before last.

This is not the first edition of the *Chronicle of the Morea.* It was published at the beginning of the last century by Buchon. But the Schmitt edition is more scientific, and more meticulous, through its comparison of existing manuscripts.

For a long time the great question was whether the Greek text of the *Chronicle* was a translation from the French. Professor Schmitt holds that it is not, and that the Greek poem is the original. In support of this view, he writes, among other things, "What need had the Greeks to translate into their language a work expressing such a ferocious hatred for their race? But that such a work should have been written in Greek by some Hellenized Frank does not strike one as peculiar."

The name of the author of the *Chronicle* has not been preserved. Nevertheless, the persistent antipathy he expresses toward the Greeks, and his persistent sympathy for the Franks, make it safe to assume that he was a Frank, or the child of a Frankish father and a Greek mother.

He appears to have been a notary, or at least to have been connected to the civil authority, to judge by the exactitude and relish with which he describes the feudal customs, the decisions and the procedure[1] of the courts, and the familiarity he demonstrates with treaties and contracts. On the other hand, when it comes to

1. In English in the original.

military details his interest seems to flag, and either he summarizes them, or leaves them out altogether, remarking, "Why should I tell you all this, which bores even me," or, "Why should I go over this again so as to bore you all the more," or, "Why should I tell you all this and when would I ever write it?"

From a literary standpoint, the *Chronicle of the Morea* has little to offer. One praiseworthy aspect is the clarity of its style, with here and there a touch of the poetic.

The *Chronicle* begins with a kind of prologue in which the author narrates the events surrounding the capture of Constantinople by the Franks. He then passes on to his proper subject, the conquest of the Peloponnese.

At the beginning of the thirteenth century the situation in the Peloponnese was such as to make the work of the foreign conquerors considerably easier. The confusion of powers was at its height; and the local powers fought among themselves in an attempt to increase their influence and extend their domains. Yet for all that, the land was not poor. Geoffroy de Villehardouin, addressing a friend from the nobility, writes, "I come from a land of great abundance, which they call the Morea" (*The Conquest of Constantinople*, Edition Bouchet, i). Sixty or seventy years before that Edrises, a learned Arab, had traveled through the Peloponnese, and he too portrays it as rich and populous. He mentions that it had thirteen sizeable cities, of which the most important were Corinth, Patras, and another which he calls Arcadia.

The author of the *Chronicle*, an admirer of the Frankish knights, announces with great importance that he will be telling us the "deeds of champions," and adds:

> [I]f you have the desire to hear the deeds of good soldiers, to learn and be instructed, perhaps you will attain your wish. If you know letters, start reading; if, on the other hand, you are illiterate, sit down beside me and listen; and I hope, if you are wise, that you will benefit, for many who have come after them have made much progress because of the tales of those of old. [1349–55][2]

The first of these champions was Guillaume de Champlitte. Champlitte was the brother of the Duke of Champagne, who was killed while on crusade in Syria. When news of the Duke's death reached France, one of his brothers inherited the duchy,

---

2. English translations of passages from the *Chronicle* are taken from Harold E. Lurier, ed. and trans., *Crusaders as Conquerors: The Chronicle of the Morea,* (New York: Columbia University Press, 1964.) The line numbers provided are from that edition.

while the other, Guillaume, took a large sum of money from their common funds, mobilized cohorts, and departed for Romania with the aim of "conquering some castles and tracts of land, and holding them as his *igonika* [hereditary estate]."

The territory of Romania in which the adventurer sought his *igonika* was the Peloponnese. He disembarked in Achaia and attacked Patras, which surrendered at once, without resistance. Andravida also surrendered. After these successes he set out for Corinth where, however, the Greeks—under the strong leadership of Sgouros—put up a stiff fight.

The Franks sacked the town of Corinth, and the Greeks withdrew to the castle. Added to this, Boniface, the king of Salonica, descended on the Peloponnese and, upon meeting with Guillaume, recognized him as sovereign of a great part of the Peloponnese, as well as granting him feudal rights over Athens, Euboia, and Voustitsa.

But as much as Guillaume loved his Greek dominions, once word came that his brother had died and that he had inherited the Duchy of Champagne in France, he made up his mind to leave, and while maintaining his rights of sovereignty over the Peloponnese, he relinquished authority to Geoffroy de Villehardouin.

One striking detail in the poet's narrative is the ease with which, by his account, the Peloponnesians submitted. With emphasis and satisfaction he depicts their surrender, first in Andravida:

> and after they had come close to Andravida and the Andravisaioi learned that the Franks were coming, the archons and the commons of the town of Andravida went out with the crosses and the ikons and went to do homage to the Champenois. And he, as an all-prudent man, received them well, and he swore and promised them he would not act unjustly towards them, nor would they receive damage to their estates, but would have honor, gifts, and great beneficences; all swore to him that they would die his slaves (1432–41)

then in Corinthian territory:

> the archons and likewise the commons began to go up, small and great, from the town of Damala and from as far away as Hagion Oros; all who heard of it went with great eagerness and swore to the Champenois to die as his slaves; and he received them with great joy. (1496–1501)

[The manuscript ends here.]